Uncovering Japanese Mythology

Exploring the Ancient Stories, Legends, and Folktales of the Land of the Rising Sun

Lucas Russo

Table of Contents

Introduction

Japanese mythology and folklore have been food for inspiration and fascination for years, if not decades. It was transmitted to the Western world through translations, books, anime, manga, and feature films. And yet, in the general consciousness, the understanding of Japanese mythology, folklore, and the system of beliefs that stood and still stands behind it, is still only perfunctory.

In this book, I want to show you not only a selection of the most fascinating stories from Japanese folklore—and there is no shortage of those—but also to acquaint you with the most important Japanese deities, and to help you understand the religious principles that stand behind the belief in many of the entities and supernatural creatures, as well as the Japanese philosophy of life. Culturally, Japan has been in a rather unique position in comparison to other civilizations from the region, and from the rest of the world: With its ages of political isolationism and its characteristic set of religious beliefs stemming from Shintoism and the Japanese version of Buddhism, it created a very particular climate for the development of myths and folktales. A climate that differs from the one we are used to with various mythologies originating in Europe. As a result, the mythology that stemmed from these specific cultural circumstances—and which will be the main focus of this book—is also highly original.

So let us begin our journey. First, we will try to understand Japanese religious beliefs and historical social structure better: The principles behind Shintoism and how Buddhism arrived in Japan; the divine status of the Japanese emperor, and the meaning of the social classes. But most importantly, we will explore the rich world of numerous Japanese deities, supernatural creatures, and heroes—and we will learn the stories pertaining to them. We will learn about the creation of the world and the islands in the Japanese archipelago; about the powerful Sun goddess and volatile gods of the storm; and finally, about regular, impoverished people who encountered supernatural beings in numerous Japanese fairy tales.

I hope that you will enjoy this rich world of myth that Japan has to offer. From the highest of gods to the lowest of people, there is something in this mythology for everyone.

Chapter 1:

The Foundation of Myth

Shinto and Japanese Buddhism were two cornerstones upon which Japanese mythology was built, and they are crucial for its understanding. In this chapter, we will learn the principles standing behind each of these traditions. We will also explore Japan's historic political structure, as well as develop a basic understanding of the antiquity of Japanese tradition and how it changed throughout history—as a better understanding of the Japanese social structure might prove very useful in understanding the plot points of folktales. Treat this chapter as a compendium and an introduction: A guide that you will take on your journey.

Shinto—Religion From Japan

Shinto is a religion that differs a lot from the most popular monotheistic religions such as Christianity or Islam. First of all, it is polytheistic, holding a belief in many divine beings; but it's also animistic—meaning that it ascribes divine properties and spiritual essence to animals, places, and even objects. This special nature of Shintoism is also the most defining feature behind Japanese mythology: Although many Japanese gods can be distinguished as such, the line between a god and a spirit or a semi-divine being can be blurry. Additionally, the animistic aspect of Shinto means that everyday objects, places, and animals would acquire supernatural status—something that we will look at more closely in Chapter 6.

Moreover, Shinto has no single canon of texts and versions of beliefs; instead, beliefs vary and can often contradict each other. In this, Shintoism is similar to many decentralized polytheistic religions; but in contrast to many of them, the sheer number of mythical beings and gods in which the followers of Shinto could believe is much larger. It is not just that there are different versions of the same gods in different regions of Japan; it's also that some of the gods only preside over tiny dominions, in one or two regions only. In fact, the decentralization of Shinto is so great that the only unifying feature that could describe this religion as a whole is the belief in kami, or, supernatural entities (meaning both gods, spirits, and other, less specified powers) (Cali et al., 2013).

Some scholars have described Shinto as less of a religion, and more of a philosophy or a way of life (Picken, 1994; Cali et al., 2013). Unlike many modern Western religions,

Shinto isn't exclusive and allows for the practice of other religious beliefs alongside it. Over the ages, many non-Japanese religious beliefs have infiltrated Shinto; Buddhism is perhaps the most prominent of these influences, but so are Chinese Confucianism and Taoism.

There are different types of Shinto, from the more official version centered around shrines to the more private one, practiced by individual people. Historically, there was also the official state version of the religion, emphasizing the divine status of the Japanese emperor and enacting financial control over Shinto temples. This, of course, is no longer the case in modern-day Japan.

Given that Shinto is so relaxed and decentralized, is there any set of beliefs, besides the broadest belief in the kami, that can be pointed out as characteristic of that religion? Perhaps the most defining feature of Shinto and one that can be found the most surprising to the Western mentality is the lack of clear division between good and evil. The kami can encompass both good fortune and destruction, and there is no reward for "good deeds" in the afterlife. In fact, Shinto is more concentrated on life rather than on what might come after it; some believers hold that the dead assist the living as ghosts, and others adopt more Buddhist afterlife beliefs (Littleton, 2002);

but in any case, Shinto emphasizes life and adaptability to its ever-changing circumstances.

However, instead of good and evil, Shinto distinguishes between purity and impurity. Humans are considered intrinsically pure; however, they can become impure through contact with death or disease, or through practicing cultural taboos such as incest or bestiality; menstruation and childbirth can also cause impurity (Nelson, 2006). There are many rituals aimed at purification, and some of them are an imitation of the rites that some of the kami are believed to have undergone when faced with similar challenges.

Shinto does not have a single code of conduct. Some of the qualities that are emphasized as desirable for its followers include honesty and adherence to truth, frankness, hard work, and giving thanks to the kami (Picken, 2011). This list of precepts is general enough that historically, it could be applied to many varying social and political circumstances—and as we will see in later chapters, it also influenced the rather vague morality behind Japanese folktales.

Today, Shintoism tends to veer toward general conservatism and valuing Japan's national interests.

Japanese Buddhism

Buddhism first arrived in Japan around the 6th century C.E. The Silk Road—the trade route that connected India to China and Korea—had its extension in the maritime route between Japan and Korea and China. As such, the Japanese version of Buddhism was already filtered through the Chinese and Korean versions of the religion when it arrived on the archipelago. According to one of the chronicles of Japan, the *Nihon Shoki*, the Japanese emperor Soga no Iname (506–570) allowed only one Japanese clan (the Soga clan) to adopt Buddhism, in order to see how the worship would affect his subjects and if the Japanese kami would be furious (Deal & Ruppert, 2015).

As a result, the Soga clan became the staunchest champions of Buddhism, even though they initially faced a lot of opposition, and sometimes even outright hostility. Over the years and throughout the rule of different imperial dynasties in Japan, Buddhism was more or less accepted and endorsed by the state. Often, this was tied to general strong cultural influences from Korea and China, which, at various points in history, were considered more sophisticated; thus, Chinese technology and poetry found their way to Japan. Along with Buddhist practices, the art, and architecture tied to that religion were also introduced. Fascinatingly,

Buddhism became a religious vehicle for cultural exchange spanning thousands of kilometers: Some of the Japanese Buddhism iconographies can trace its roots as far as Hellenistic-Indian depictions, which allows us to find a common style between ancient Greek sculpture and Japanese sculpture (Tanabe, 2003).

But apart from artistic influences, what was the religious importance of Buddhism in Japan? Today, Japanese Buddhism mainly centers around one Buddha. But historically, as Buddha was a name applied to a category of those who have attained awakening or nirvana, rather than to a singular person, over 3,000 Buddhas were worshiped in Japan (Nukariya, 2016). This ties to the local Japanese Shinto traditions with its multiplicity of gods.

Moreover, the Japanese Buddhist pantheon was hierarchical. There were six levels of deities (the first level being the highest, and the sixth the lowest): The Buddhas (those who attained enlightenment), the Bodhisattvas (those who attained enlightenment but have chosen to stay on earth and spread the knowledge of Buddhism), Wisdom Kings (powerful gods who can influence reality), Heavenly Deities (gods who go through a cycle of rebirths and strive to attain nirvana, therefore try to help the followers of Buddhism), Circumstantial Appearances (protective forces which are mostly Shinto gods adopted for Buddhist purposes), and finally, Religious Masters (influential historical figures).

There are numerous schools of Buddhism in Japan, both historically and contemporarily. Although some of them are esoteric (based on hidden teachings), all emphasize attaining enlightenment, thus filling the gap in the Shintoist lack of belief in any form of afterlife. Moreover, they add new concepts and deities to the already enormous pantheon of Japanese gods.

Japanese State

Both Shintoism and Buddhism were religions used by the Japanese state to reinforce order and obedience to the emperor. But what was the societal structure of Japan? How did it change throughout the centuries? And, most importantly, how did it influence the Japanese system of beliefs?

Brief Chronology

Before we talk at length about the organization of the Japanese state, it's worth mentioning the chronology of Japan's history; after all, the culture hardly stayed the same throughout over 1,500 years of its development.

Jōmon Period (ca. 13000–1000 B.C.E.)

Although human activity on the Japanese archipelago reaches paleolithic times, the first signs of a complex culture can be dated to this period. The people of that time slowly changed from hunter-gatherers to a sedentary culture and started creating elaborately decorated pottery. Not much more is known about them, however.

Yayoi Period (ca. 1000 B.C.E.–ca. 240 C.E.)

The period is named after the Yayoi People, who migrated to the Japanese archipelago from China and Korea, transforming the culture that they encountered. Most prominently, they introduced the cultivation of rice, as well as bronze and iron weapons. Traditionally, the first legendary emperor of Japan, Emperor Jimmu, was believed to have ruled in this era, in the 7th and 6th century B.C.E.

Around 82 C.E., a Chinese chronicle called the *Book of Han*, was created; it contains the first known mention of Japan as an entity divided into as many as a hundred kingdoms. A later Chinese work, *Wei Zhi* from the 3rd century C.E., mentions that around 240 C.E., one of the Japanese kingdoms gained power over the others and the unification process began (Sansom, 1982). The kingdom's name was said to be Yamatai, and it was supposed to be ruled by a semi-mythical empress and shamaness, Himiko.

Kofun Period (ca. 250–538)

The first serious unification attempt arrived with the Kofun period of Japanese history when several previously independent kingdoms united under a single territory. The word *kofun* refers to a style of burial mounds that are most characteristic of this period. It also saw the development of the three oldest Shinto shrines in Japan: The Nagata Shrine, Hirota Shrine, and Ikuta Shrine.

Asuka Period (538–710)

The Asuka Period started what is known today as Classical Japan. Its most defining feature was the introduction of Buddhism by the Soga clan which then controlled Japan for much of this age. The clan was overthrown in 645 by the Fujiwara clan, who introduced extensive reforms to government, based on Chinese structures of power and on the spirit of Confucianism. Overall, the Asuka Period saw large Chinese cultural influences on Japan.

Nara Period (710–794)

The Nara Period was very important for the construction of Japanese mythology. During this time, two legendary accounts, the books of *Kojiki* and *Nihon Shoki*, were created; they describe the Japanese creation myth and explain the descendance of Japanese rulers from the gods.

Unfortunately, this period was also characterized by some natural disasters, including famines and disease, which led to a more forceful promotion of Buddhism as a way to appease the higher powers by increasing the piousness in the people.

Heian Period (794–1185)

The Heian Period was one of the most important in Japanese history. The government, controlled largely by the Fujiwara clan, wasn't the strongest at the time, with most land outside of the capital being controlled by private landowners; on the other hand, this period also saw major cultural and artistic developments at the imperial court. The Chinese influence declined and more sophisticated forms of Japanese script were developed.

The period ended with a succession dispute which then led to a civil war, a result of which was the seizing of power by the shogun Minamoto no Yoritomo. This marked the symbolic end of Classical Japan and the beginning of Feudal Japan, a time period that is perhaps the best-known to non-Japanese readers.

Kamakura Period (1185–1333)

This period was characterized by the consolidation of power and the rule of the military class (the shogunate) which would last for centuries to come. The hierarchical social structure, which we will talk about in a bit, was largely created during this time. The shogun, or the military dictator, remained practically the most important person in the country, and the principles of the samurai army were developed. Politically, this period saw two invasions of the Mongols, in 1274 and 1281, respectively. Although these invasions ended in an eventual Japanese victory, the wars exhausted the state's finances, leading to the discontent of the samurai who were poorly compensated for their fighting. This led to a series of rebellions which eventually resulted in the end of the Kamakura Period and the start of the Muromachi Period.

Muromachi Period (1333–1568)

The Muromachi Period saw the split between Southern and Northern Japan, as a result of a revolt and civil war. It was a period of violent strife and disobedience of the feudal magnates, called the daimyōs, to the shogunate.

But it was also the time when the first Europeans arrived in Japan. In 1543, Portuguese traders mistakenly set off course and arrived at Japanese shores. This would start a trade exchange which would also play a part in the period of anarchy; for example, European muskets would be introduced to the Japanese army (Farris, 2009).

But the Europeans also started missionary work. In the second half of the 16th century, the first Jesuits were allowed to settle in some Japanese villages and to convert their inhabitants to Christianity. However, Christian beliefs and missionary streak often clashed with Japanese culture, resulting in the Jesuits' expulsion from many areas.

Despite the civil war and anarchy, the Muromachi Period saw a large uptake in population and a flourishment of trade. Some of the most characteristic Japanese art forms were developed during that time, such as ink wash painting, the creation of the bonsai trees, and Noh, a type of a dance-drama (Perez, 1998).

Azuchi-Momoyama Period (1568–1600)

The relatively short Azuchi-Momoyama Period was characterized by the consolidation of power and the restriction put upon the daimyōs, as well as by persecution of the previously tolerated Christians. The most prominent ruler from this time, the warlord

Toyotomi Hideyoshi, led many aggressive campaigns against Korea and China. However, the war ended right after his death, and, after some strife, the throne passed to Hideyoshi's former ally, the shogun Tokugawa Ieyasu, who started a new era: The famous Edo Period.

Edo Period (1600–1868)

The Edo Period was a time of peace and prosperity. The Tokugawa shogunate maintained social order and restricted the influence of the daimyōs, but often at a very harsh price: The death penalties were often very brutal (for instance, death by boiling). It was also during that time that the concept of seppuku, the ancient practice of suicide, was ritualized and presented as an alternative punishment for those belonging to the nobility.

It was also during that time when a new policy, that of Japan's isolationism, was implemented. After the times of unrest, all foreign influences were seen as a threat. Thus, effectively, foreign trade as well as sea travel were banned, and previous foreign influences were uprooted (Christianity was banned as a whole in 1638). The only exception to the foreign trade ban were the Dutch who were allowed to trade at Nagasaki (*Dejima Nagasaki*, 2013).

During the Edo Period, the population of Japan doubled, reaching thirty million (Totman, 2014). The capital of the country, Edo (modern-day Tokyo), was the largest city in the world (Henshall, 2012). It was also a time of the development of the merchant class which, having accumulated more and more wealth, became the patrons of the arts. Cultural concepts such as the haiku (a short form of poetry), and the institution of a geisha (a professional entertainer—not a prostitute!) were developed.

As the years went by and the Japanese society changed, the shogunate slowly declined in power. The merchant class was more and more prominent and the peasantry was growing discontent, especially after a series of famines in the early 19th century. Even the samurai slowly grew disillusioned with the rulers. At the same time, the only window that Japan had to the West— through the Dutch traders—brought new ideas and ideologies to the archipelago, sparking interest among the intellectuals.

In 1853, the American fleet commanded by Commodore Matthew C. Perry forcefully arrived at Japan's shores, aiming to end the country's isolationism. The ships were equipped with guns, against which the Japanese forces were helpless; in the end, the Americans forced the Japanese to agree to let them replenish their ships with provisions and to trade with the Americans in the future. It was a veritable cultural clash, and Japan was in turmoil.

Many Japanese people were angered by the shogunate's inability to repel the American 'barbarians.' Nationalistic sentiments grew, and in 1868, the young emperor Meiji was forced to end the Tokugawa shogunate.

Meiji Period (1868–1912)

The Meiji Period could be classified as the first period of Modern Japan. It was characterized by the rule of the oligarchs, with the emperor holding only nominal power. The oligarchs sought to transform Japan so that it could stand equal among the Western superpowers. The class system was abolished and the daimyōs' domains were changed into prefectures; the ban on Christianity was lifted. Institutions for scientific research were established, and even in terms of clothing and hairstyle, the Japanese started following the Europeans. Western literary styles were adopted, which sparked a wave of prose writing. This allowed for the inventive and fascinating nature, merging of the traditional Japanese and Western storytelling practices. It was also a time of rapid economic growth.

The Meiji Period also saw Japan's military expansion. Through conflicts with Taiwan and Russia, the country expanded into the Japanese Empire.

Taishō Period (1912–1926)

During that short period, the importance of the Japanese Empire on the political map grew. Japan also adopted Western democratic institutions, although political dissidents would also be penalized harshly. In terms of culture, this was a time when Japanese prose was more and more widely read and further developed.

However, the death of Emperor Taishō marked the end of the period, giving way to the longest reign in Japanese history—that of Emperor Hirohito.

Shōwa Period (1926–1989)

The beginning of Emperor Hirogito's reign was marked by a growing popularity of nationalistic movements in Japan, which resulted in the country's turn to fascism—and in the end, with Japan's involvement in World War II on the side of Nazi Germany. Even before the war, Japan's expansionist tendencies resulted in some truly deplorable actions, such as the massacre of Chinese civilians in Nanjing during the Second Sino-Japanese War in 1937.

In 1945, after the lost world war and the absolutely disastrous consequences of the dropping of two atomic bombs on Hiroshima and Nagasaki by the Allies, Japan was in tatters. The Empire of Japan was dismantled in

1947, and from 1945 to 1952, the country was occupied by the Allied forces. Under their rule, Japan underwent drastic changes: Political power was decentralized; the country was demilitarized; and further democratic reforms followed. Emperor Hirohito was forced to denounce his divine nature in return for the allowance to keep his power. This was a massive cultural and religious shift in Japan's consciousness.

From the 1950s onward, Japan experienced rapid economic growth. Moreover, it remained an ally of the United States during the Cold War. Further cultural developments were made most notably, cinema flourished.

Heisei Period and Reiwa Period (1989–present)

The last two periods of Japan's recent history, marked by the reign of Emperor Akihito from 1989 to 2019 and Emperor Naruhito from 2019 to this day, saw further economic growth for Japan, despite a temporary setback in the 1990s. Culturally, it was—and still is—a time of development and thriving of Japanese popular culture, with its manga, anime, and video games—many of which use motifs from traditional Japanese folklore. Today, Japan is one of the technological champions in the world, even if some of its political decisions, especially regarding its relations with China in the past, remain controversial (Henshall, 2012).

All in all, Japan underwent an incredible journey: From the feudal society that it remained way into the 19th century, to the modern technological power. This change we'll later see reflected in its myths and folk stories, which carry on way beyond the end of feudalism and traditional values.

Traditional Social Structure

The traditional and most iconic social structure that we often have in mind when we think about historical Japan, is that of the Edo Period; and that is also the structure we will talk about here. This model of society will be later reflected in many traditional Japanese tales.

The social hierarchy during the Tokugawa shogunate somehow resembled a pyramid. The Emperor, of course, was on the very top of that structure; however, for most of the period, his rule was only nominal, even if he claimed descendance from the gods. The real ruler of Japan was the shogun—the military commander.

Yet still above the shogun were the kuge: The court nobility. They were civil servants whose positions were prestigious and held cultural significance, but similarly to the emperor, their power was very restricted. They would often be, however, patrons of the arts.

Below the kuge was the shogun—the actual ruler of Japan. He was de facto a military dictator who oversaw all comings and goings in the country. The title was hereditary, and it remained in the hands of the Tokugawa clan for the duration of the Edo Period.

Below the shogun were the already mentioned daimyō. They were magnates and landowners, responsible for the administration of their domains and being the most prominent members of the military class. They, in fact, controlled the vastest areas in the country.

Almost all the rest of the Japanese society was grouped below the daimyō and were divided into four groups: The samurai (warriors), peasants (or farmers), artisans, and merchants. The samurai were the most prestigious and highest-standing of these groups, and were considered nobles. They would be employed by their daimyō, and their warfare would be restricted by a number of honor-based rules, which often turned warfare into artform rather than simple skill. Among the samurai themselves, there were also ones of higher and lower standing.

Importantly, the peasants were esteemed in Japanese society. After all, they produced food and were the backbone of the country's proper functioning. However, the peasants were mostly tied to their villages and required a permit in order to travel outside. Still, they owned the land they farmed, even if it would often be taxed by the local daimyō.

Artisans, as the producers of non-essential goods, were placed below the peasants. They mostly lived in cities and produced items that would later be bought by the nobility.

Finally, the merchants were the lowest of classes—as those who traded, but they did not produce any goods. Like the artisans, they lived in cities, and would often be disregarded—however, as we have already mentioned, their numbers steadily grew during the Edo Period and as time passed, they gained more and more power, despite the laws that restricted them from displaying their wealth too overtly.

Below all the social classes was a group of people regarded as untouchable. Those were people who performed jobs in some way related to death—such as undertakers, butchers, or executioners—and therefore, according to the Shinto principles, were perpetually impure. Ethnic minorities were also excluded from the class structure. Those people would be actively discriminated against and live in their own ghettos, isolated from the rest of the population.

Chapter 2:

The Origin Story

The Creation of Takamagahara

According to *Kojiki* and *Nihon Shoki*, the world was created from chaos. In the beginning, there was nothing but this chaos, and everything was silent. The chaos itself was a tangle of particles that finally started moving around, causing the lightest ones to float upwards and the heaviest to fall downwards.

The light was a result of the lightest particles grouping on top of the universe. Below, the heavier particles formed clouds which then created Takamagahara, "the High Plane of Heaven," which would later become the realm of all gods. The heaviest particles, for their part, fell way down, creating the Earth (Chamberlain, 2008).

The realm of Takamagahara was a sacred one. Later, it would be connected to the Earth by a special bridge, called the Ame-no-ukihashi ("the Floating Bridge of Heaven"). For now though, it gave birth to the first gods:

The Kotoamatsukami, who would later disappear and not take part in any other myths and legends.

The first three deities who appeared from the Heavens were Amenominakanushi (Central Master), Takamimusubi (High Creator), and Kamimusubi (Divine Creator). After them, Umashiashikabihikoji (Energy) and Amenotokotachi (Heaven) appeared. None of these deities had a fixed gender or a partner, and their creation was spontaneous. Immediately after their emergence, they hid themselves from view. Those mysterious deities wouldn't be widely recognized, nor worshiped outside of the creation story.

The Emergence of New Gods

But then, new gods emerged from the universe. Later, they would collectively be known as Kamiyonanayo, or, the seven generations of the kami—the Shinto gods. They appeared in the following order:

First came Kuni-no-Tokotachi and Toyokumono. Like the older gods, those deities emerged spontaneously, and their appearance is likened to a reed growing out of the soil. They didn't have partners, either, nor did they have gender. They also hid themselves almost immediately.

Next came subsequent pairs of male-female gods who were consorts as well as siblings: Uhijini and Suhijini; Tsunuguhi and Ikuguhi; Ōtonoji and Ōtonobe; Omodaru and Aya-kashiko-ne; and finally, Izanagi and Izanami. It is that last pair that would play an important role in Japanese mythology: It is the pair of creator gods who gave birth to a number of other important deities, as well as organized the Earth, lifted it from the chaos, and created the Japanese archipelago.

How did Izanagi and Izanami achieve all this? When they were born, the Earth was chaotic and was drifting on the water like floating oil (Chamberlain, 2008). The gods were tasked with solidifying its shape. For this purpose, they used the Amenonuhoko, a spear laid with jewels. They stirred the chaos with the spear and gathered all the landmass together. The dripping matter that fell from the tip of the spear when the task was done, formed a small island called Onogoro. It was a mythical place where later, Izanagi and Izanami descended and erected a large stone pillar. They realized that their task was now to be married and to have children; so in the first-ever marriage ceremony, they walked in the opposite direction of the pillar, and got married when they walked around the whole island and met each other in the middle again. Later, Izanagi and Izanami would create a palace on Onogoro.

Then, they had their first child: Hiruko (or Ebisu), the God of fishermen and good luck. He was imperfect, born without bones. This was the result of an initial blunder between his parents during their marriage ceremony, Izanami spoke first, even though it was the man, Izanagi, who was supposed to have precedence.

So Hiruko was put on a reed boat and set afloat. Later, he would be washed ashore and would find foster parents, thanks to whom he would overcome his disability; we will talk about him in the next chapter.

But meanwhile, Izanagi and Izanami decided to repeat their marriage ceremony. This time, Izanagi spoke first and the union was successful. Several islands of the Japanese archipelago were born from it, including Awaji Island, Shikoku, Oki Islands, Kyushu, Iki, Tsushima, Sado, and Honshu. The next task was to beget the gods who would populate these islands. So, Izanami gave birth to three more children: The sun goddess Amaterasu, the moon god Tsukuyomi-no-Mikoto, and Susanoo-no-Mikoto, the contrary god of storms. Unfortunately, after giving birth numerous times, Izanami's body grew tired. She finally died giving birth to Kagutsuchi, the god of fire.

Izanagi couldn't bear the grief that this brought him. In his rage, he struck Kagutsuchi, beheading him, and then cut his body into eight pieces. The chunks of

Kagutsuchi's body became volcanoes, from which emerged new gods, born of Kagutsuchi's remains mixed with Izanagi's tears: Watatsumi, the water dragon; Kuraokami, the ice dragon; Takemikazuchi, the god of thunder; Futsunuchi, the warrior god; Amatsumikaboshi, a malevolent trickster god; and finally, Ōyamatsumi, the god of mountains, sea, and war.

The death of Izanami marked the end of the creation process and was the first death of any being. Izanagi now descended into Yomi, a mythical island of the dead. He hoped to see Izanami again and, possibly, to resurrect her. There was only one condition, he couldn't look at her when he led her from the Underworld.

Unfortunately, Izanami had already eaten food that was served to her on the land, and therefore, couldn't leave it. When Izanagi heard of this, his anger grew and he broke the only condition set upon him. He lit his torch and raised it to see Izanami's face one more time… Only to drop it with horror when he realized that his wife was now a rotting corpse.

Horrified, Izanagi fled from Yomi. Izanami, ashamed of having been seen in such a decaying state, sent several gods of thunder after him, but Izanagi distracted them and fled. We will learn what happened to him later in the next chapter; for now, the history of the world's creation was finished, and the history of the world began.

Jimmu, the First Emperor

Even though the legend of Emperor Jimmu has no place in the story of the creation of the world, it's an important origin story of the Japanese state—and a legend that for ages has served Japanese emperors as the explanation of their legitimacy. The chronicles of *Kojiki* and *Nihon Shoki* cite the dates of his reign as 660–585 B.C.E.: Right in the middle of the Yayoi Period. Today, historians mostly agree that Jimmu was a legendary figure rather than a historical one; however, some of the events in which he was supposed to be involved might be a reflection of actual wars and migrations of peoples to the Japanese archipelago (Henshall, 2014).

According to the legendary accounts, Jimmu was the descendant of the gods: His father was Ugayafukiaezu, a god and a grandson of Ninigi-no-Mikoto, who had been sent to govern Japan by the sun goddess, Amaterasu, herself one of the numerous children of Izanagi and Izanami. In turn, Jimmu's mother was Tamayori-hime, also a goddess. Jimmu was then semi-divine, and his reign would mark the beginning of human history and the end of the gods' rule over the Earth.

Jimmu had three younger brothers: Hikoitsuse, Inai, and Mikeirino, and one older brother, Itsuse no Mikoto. They were all born on the island of Kyushu, the southernmost part of the Japanese archipelago. This was not a good strategic spot for ruling the country, however; so they decided to migrate.

Initially, Itsuse no Mikoto led the migration. The brothers traveled through the Seto Inland Sea, reaching Naniwa (today's Osaka). However, it was already occupied and ruled by a chieftain called Nagasunehiko, who had very long legs. A battle ensued, during which Itsuse no Mikoto was killed, and the brothers lost. Too late, Jimmu realized that the reason for their defeat had been that they had been facing the sun while fighting, which blinded them and rendered them clumsy.

Jimmu now took over as a chieftain. He commanded his forces to move to the Kii Peninsula and, later, to the Kumano Region, from where his army was more strategically positioned as the sun shone on their backs rather than their faces. The second battle was victorious and Nagasunehiko was killed.

Now, Jimmu's forces moved to the Yamato Province. A divine guide was sent by Takamimusubi, the god of agriculture, to aid them on their way: It was a mythical three-legged crow called Yatagarasu, who was also the incarnation of the sun.

In Yamato, Jimmu's forces defeated an ethnic group known as the Emishi. The chieftain of Yamato,

Nigihayahi, though he used to be an ally of Nagasunehiko, accepted Jimmu's rule. Jimmu ascended the throne and became the first emperor of the whole of Japan.

But Japan didn't have a name. One day, as Jimmu was climbing the Nara mountain, from which top he planned to chart the country and the Seto Inland Sea, he noticed a curious phenomenon: Dragonflies were mating on the top of the mountain, creating heart shapes from their bodies. As Jimmu was observing this, a mosquito suddenly flew close to him and landed on his arm, intent on biting him and stealing some of his royal blood. But immediately, one of the dragonflies flew to Jimmu's defense and killed the mosquito. Grateful for this deed, Jimmu named the Japanese islands the Dragonfly Islands, which in ancient Japanese read *Akitsushima*.

According to the legend, Jimmu's reign was a long and peaceful one. He was supposed to have died when 126 years old. He is the protoplast of the Imperial House of Japan, also known as the House of Yamato, which nominally rules Japan to this day.

Chapter 3:

Gods

Given the nature of Shinto, the list of deities that can be found in the Japanese tradition is nearly endless. In this chapter, I will present to you a long, but not nearly complete compendium of the most interesting and important Japanese gods; in the next chapter, we will learn about the goddesses. This overview will include deities from ancient times, as well as those who are still present in Japanese folklore and urban myths to this day. It will also include Shinto gods as well as Buddhist deities.

Aizen Myō-ō

The first god on our list is a Buddhist deity. Also known as Rāgarāja, he is worshiped in the esoteric Buddhist tradition, especially that coming from China. He is one of the Wisdom Kings—the third level of the Buddhist hierarchy of deities and spiritual beings.

Rāgarāja's task is to transform an individual's earthly desires, especially love, and lust, into spiritual awakening. He is most commonly depicted as a red-skinned man sitting cross-legged in a lotus position, with three pairs of hands. The expression on his face is fierce, and he often possesses a third eye and hair made of flames. They represent the burning feeling of rage and lust. Despite Rāgarāja's propensity of liberating and transforming earthly desires, Buddhist followers would often pray to him asking for good luck in love and marriage. In Japan, he is also known to protect the shores from any invaders from the sea. As such, he was especially popular during the Heian Period, when he was especially revered by the lower classes (Goepper, 1993).

Ajisukitakahikone

Ajisukitakahikone is a Shinto god (kami) of agriculture and thunder. His thunderous tendencies were uncovered when his close friend and brother-in-law, Ame-no-Wakahiko, died. When Ajiksukitakahikone came to his funeral, he was mistakenly taken for his deceased friend brought back to life, as they had looked very much alike. Enraged that he had just been connected to a dead man (and therefore made impure), Ajiksukitakahikone drew his sword and destroyed the hut where the funeral was being held, and then kicked it, transforming it into the

Moyama mountain in Mino province. Then, Ajiksukitakahikone flew away, and so great was his anger that it lit up the sky.

Amatsu-Mikaboshi

Amatsu-Mikaboshi was one of the gods that emerged from the mutilated body of Kagutsuchi. Not much is known about him except for the fact that he was malicious in nature and always rebelled against the authority of the other gods. During the Asuka and Nara Periods, when Chinese Buddhist influences on Japan were the strongest, Amatsu-Mikaboshi became a personification of Venus. This, later, would lead to a new description of his nature: He was now the god of all stars, less malicious, subdued by his brother, Takemikazuchi, the god of thunder.

Amatsumara

Amatsumara is the god of blacksmiths. He resides in the realm of the gods, Takamagahara, where he is the blacksmith of the gods.

We have only one myth pertaining to Amatsumara: One day, the sun goddess Amaterasu, angered by her brother

Susanoo, hid in a cave, depriving the Earth of her light. A plan had to be devised in order to lure her out: So, the god of wisdom, Omoikane, devised a plan.

He ordered Amatsumara to make a beautiful mirror. Then, they hung it in the tree, which they also decorated heavily. Preparations were made for a holy celebration, and the goddess of joy, Ame-no-Uzume-no-Mikoto was brought to a state of holy frenzy. This caused her to bare her breasts and genitals which, in turn, made the gods laugh.

When Amaterasu heard the rumble of laughter, she was intrigued and mildly annoyed. Why were the gods so happy when she wasn't among them? So she called out from her cave, asking what all the fuss was about.

One of the gods responded that the deities were happy because they had just discovered a goddess who was even better than Amaterasu. At this, the sun goddess couldn't contain herself anymore; she pushed away the boulder that was barring the entrance to the cave and peeked out.

The gods acted instantly; they immediately placed Amatsumara's mirror in front of Amaterasu. Dazzled at her own reflection and clearly thinking that this was the new, greater goddess, Amaterasu became distracted. The gods caught her hands and pulled her out of the cave, which was then immediately blocked, preventing her from going back in. And thus, with the help of Amatsumara's mirror, the Earth regained its sun.

Ame-no-Koyane

Ame-no-Koyane was regarded as the ancestor of two very powerful Japanese clans, the Nakatomi clan, and the Fujiwara clan. He served as the priest to the gods, tasked with the performance of Ukei, a special divination ritual. He also had a second job: To be a spiritual advisor of the Imperial Palace of Japan. It was Ame-no-Koyane who performed the ritual that caused the goddess Ame-no-Uzume-no-Mikoto to bare herself and, as a result, to cause Amaterasu to leave her cave.

Ame-no-Wakahiko

Ame-no-Wakahiko is the god of grain, to whom several interesting stories are tied. In one of them, it was said that he was sent by the gods to become the ruler of the Earth. He was supposed to report back to them as soon as he established his rule; however, when he descended on the Earth, he found a beautiful maiden there, fell in love, and forgot about everything.

Eight years passed, and the gods didn't hear back from Ame-no-Wakahiko. So, they sent a supernatural bird to look for him. When Ame-no-Wakahiko saw the bird, he shot it with his arrow; however, he didn't manage to kill it, and it still managed to fly back to the heavens, breast pierced. There, one of the gods saw the wounded bird, and pulled the arrow out of its breast; then, in anger, threw the arrow back to the Earth. By sheer bad luck, the arrow pierced Ame-no-Wakahiko in his sleep. He died on the spot.

We know the rest of the story: During Ame-no-Wakahiko's funeral, his best friend Ajisukitakahikone was confused with him, and as a result, destroyed Ame-no-Wakahiko's funerary hut. Ame-no-Wakahiko's body was transformed into Moyama mountain.

We also have another story tied to Ame-no-Wakahiko. It was written during the Muromachi Period and it's likely that its author was Emperor Go-Hanazono (1418–1471) (Satō, 2017). In this tale, the god resembles more a human man, albeit of noble standing.

The story goes as follows: Prince Ame-no-Wakahiko was a shapeshifter who had the power of transforming into a serpent. When he wished to get married, he sent a letter to a wealthy man, demanding that his three daughters were married to the serpent. This was a peculiar request, and the women had no idea that the serpent was the prince in disguise. Both the eldest and the middle daughter refused to marry him, but the youngest daughter consented.

A new house was built for the couple. It stood on a bank of a large pond where the serpent purportedly lived. When the youngest daughter went there after her marriage ceremony, the serpent emerged from the lake. The woman was scared, probably regretting her decision already; but the snake spoke to her, calming her down, and instructed her to cut off his head with a fingernail clipper.

She did as she was instructed, and suddenly, the snake shed its skin and a handsome young man emerged. He hid the snakeskin in a chest and then revealed to his bride that he was a powerful prince—and for a time, they lived happily together.

But an important errand demanded that Ame-no-Wakahiko leave his wife for a little while. He instructed her to wait for him and to never open the chest with the snakeskin; if she did, she would never see him again.

Nonetheless, the woman asked Ame-no-Wakahiko what she was supposed to do if he didn't come back for a long time. He told her to go search for him in Kyoto and buy a gourd from a woman who would know where he was.

The couple parted, and the woman waited. Her sisters visited her in the meantime, having learned that the repulsive snake which they had rejected was, in fact, a beautiful man. Now, they were envious and nagged their sister to open the box with the snakeskin. Even though she initially resisted, the woman finally caved in and opened the box.

Only smoke emerged from it; the skin wasn't inside. But the woman now knew that her husband was lost to her; so in a last desperate attempt, she decided to search for him, and set out for Kyoto.

In Kyoto, she bought the gourd as instructed; its vines allowed her to climb up to the realm of the heavens. There, she met several personified stars: The Evening Star, a comet, and the Pleiades. All of them tried to help her but didn't know who her husband was. Finally, she met a mysterious man sitting on a palanquin; he told her to seek a palace built of azure stone.

The woman found the palace. Inside, she found Ame-no-Wakahiko. But she wasn't safe there: Ame-no-Wakahiko's father was a demon (called an oni) and set out to kill the woman, so her husband had to magically turn her into various everyday objects in order to hide her.

But the demon was smart, and in the end, he found the woman out. He then set out four impossible tasks on her: To herd cattle numbering a thousand during one day and one night; to move a million grains of rice from one place to another; to spend a night in a house full of centipedes, and then, full of snakes.

The woman, however, was determined to get her husband back. With his help and his magic, she accomplished all of the tasks, outsmarting the demon. He was forced to allow the couple to see each other, but only once a year, during the Tanabata, the Japanese Star Festival (Satō, 2017). Thus, ended the story of the two tragic lovers.

Amenohoakari

Amenohoakari is the God of the sun and agriculture; he is also the deification of Nigihayahi, the chieftain who, according to the legend of Jimmu, accepted Jimmu's authority over Japan. There are no other stories about him preserved in the myths.

Amida Nyorai

Amida Nyorai, also known as Amitābha, is another Buddhist deity; a Buddha of longevity and pure perception. According to one story, during his life on earth, he used to be a monk named Dharmākara, who made a number of vows, aiming to create a pure world that would be governed by the rules of Buddhist enlightenment. In one of these vows, he promised to anyone who would call upon his name at the hour of their death, that they would be reborn in that perfect land.

So, from then on, Buddhist followers would aspire to travel to that westernmost land of bliss created by Amitābha. It was a land of many names, and full of bliss.

Amitābha is often depicted sitting in the lotus position, with hands directed outward and downward—a symbol indicating that his compassion and help could reach even the lowest of beings and save them from suffering.

Azumi-no-isora

Azumi-no-isora is a Shinto god of the seashore. He is, however, a lesser god, and would often be hired as a navigator on sea voyages—more of a supernatural helper than a deity in his own right.

Bishamonten

Bishamonten is the Japanese version of the Indian-Buddhist Vaiśravaṇa, one of the Four Heavenly Kings—gods who oversee the four cardinal directions. Bishamonten himself is the guardian of the North.

However, the Japanese version of the god acquired his own specific set of characteristics. He is worshiped as the god of war, clad in armor and with a spear in his hand. In his other hand, he would hold his symbolic treasury in the form of a small pagoda house.

Bishamonten is also believed to be one of the Seven Lucky Gods: A group of deities, (most of them originally Buddhist, but some of them had also been Chinese Taoists), who grew to be worshiped as the bringers of good luck. Initially, they were revered mostly by merchants who prayed to them to be successful in their trade transactions; however, today, everyone who feels such need could pray to them. Today, they are mostly worshiped as a group.

As one of the Seven Lucky Gods, Bishamonten is said to protect those who follow the rules, especially as pertaining to military honor. Apart from being a protector of warriors, he also defends holy places from all evil.

Daikokuten

Daikokuten, originally Mahākāla, is another god of Buddhist provenience, and one of the Seven Lucky Gods. He is the deity of good fortune and wealth. Originally a benevolent, but also a fearsome and powerful figure, his nature in Japanese tradition changed into that of an always-smiling, harmless god. Most Japanese depictions of Daikokuten show him smiling broadly. However, he is also considered a deity of ignorance and the simplicity of life that comes with it.

Daikokuten is especially tied to one of the Buddhist schools, erected by a monk by the name of Saichō (767–822). According to the legend, when he was building a monastery on the slopes of Mount Hiei (close to Kyoto), the god appeared to him in the form of an old man and offered him protection.

Over time, Daikokuten became conflated with a native Japanese god called Ōkuninushi (of whom we'll speak later). Both gods were depicted carrying a sack on their shoulders, most likely full of riches, and both were also, to some extent, considered gods of fertility. But sometimes, especially in folk religion, Daikokuten would be identified with the handicapped god Hiruko/Ebisu.

Unsurprisingly, Daikokuten reached his biggest popularity among the merchants, who would pray to him for good fortune in their endeavors.

Daruma

Daruma, or Bodhidharma, is the deified founder of Zen Buddhism. He is also credited with bringing a version of Buddhism into China, from where it transferred to Japan—no wonder his importance is really great. He lived in the 5th or 6th century C.E. In China, numerous legends are tied to his biography.

In Japan, Daruma became an inspiration for the so-called Daruma dolls: Round dolls made of papier-mâché, painted in bright colors (although the most popular one is red), with blank eyes which their owner is later encouraged to fill in one by one when they complete a task they set out for themselves (Punsmann, 1962). They are often gifted as a symbol of good luck, but, as might be expected, they also serve as motivation on a very human level which has nothing to do with divine intervention: Every time the doll's owner looks at the halfway-filled eyes, they are reminded of their goal.

The explanation behind the ties of a legless doll to Daruma is that, according to the legend, the monk had once sat in meditation for nine years straight, which caused his arms and legs to atrophy and fall off. Despite that extraordinary lack of awareness of bodily needs, Daruma still, however, kept falling asleep as he meditated; so after nine years, he cut off his eyelids to prevent himself from doing so—hence the doll's blank eyes.

Ebisu

We have already mentioned Ebisu/Hiruko—the handicapped first son of Izanagi and Izanami. Although he is of native Japanese origin, as a result of later Buddhist influence, he was numbered amongst the Seven Lucky Gods—the only Shinto deity to undergo such transformation.

According to the legend, when Izanagi and Izanami found out that their son was boneless and sent him adrift to the sea, he was washed ashore near Ezo (modern-day Hokkaidō), where he was cared for by the Ainu: The indigenous people from that region.

When Ebisu was three, a miracle happened: He grew his bones (or, according to different versions of the legend, his arms, and legs). He was still slightly deaf, but his life on the seashore, among the Ainu, seemed to be full of joy: He became known as "the Laughing God" and a patron of fishermen. Perhaps because of his initial handicap, Ebisu is associated with jellyfish.

Even today, among the fishing communities in Japan, a prayer to Ebisu before a day's work is commonplace. It is believed that he sometimes transforms into a shark and keeps the ocean calm and clean by washing ashore any debris. If someone pollutes the sea, Ebisu becomes enraged.

But Ebisu also has other tasks. Along with Daikokuten, he is worshiped as a patron of shopkeepers. As such, he is even sometimes depicted as Daikokuten's twin or son and apprentice.

Fudō Myōō

Fudō Myōō is a wrathful Buddhist god, one of the Wisdom Kings. Initially known in the Indian Sanskrit tradition as Acala, he became one of the most prominent deities for numerous Japanese Buddhist sects. He is depicted as a blue- or black-skinned man sitting in the lotus position, holding a lasso and a sword, with a fierce, angry expression on his face. His eyes are mismatched and he has two fangs, one directed upwards and one downwards. It's a symbol of the duality of the universe and human existence: The fang facing upwards signifies a soul's path towards enlightenment, while the one facing downwards is a path of the deities who descend on the earth to teach the people the way of true wisdom.

From his very introduction to Japan at the beginning of the 9th century, Fudō Myōō became an important deity who would be invoked as a protector of the state. His popularity grew rapidly and soon, he became the most important of all the Wisdom Kings in Japan.

Despite his fearsome appearance, it is believed that Fudō Myōō can rescue individuals, as well as the whole state, from all evil. Many miraculous stories about him delivering his worshipers from danger have been told since his introduction to Japan.

Fūjin

Fūjin, the demon-god of the wind, is one of the eldest Shinto gods (Roberts, 2010). He and his brother Raijin, the god of lightning, are believed to have emerged from Izanami's body after she died. She took the pair of them to Yomi, the Underworld, where they clung to her decaying body; but when Izanagi went to Yomi in an attempt to become reunited with his wife, and subsequently fled from there, horrified by her sight, Fūjin and Raijin escaped into the world.

Fūjin is depicted most often as a green-skinned demon with a terrifying expression and an outstretched windbag over his head.

Fukurokuju

Fukurokuju is one of the Seven Lucky Gods. However, he wasn't originally borrowed from the Sanskrit tradition, but from the Chinese Taoist star god Shou, who was believed to have been a human before his incarnation into a god: A hermit who could live without eating.

Fukurokuju is both the god of the stars—especially of the southern polar star—and of wisdom and longevity. He is depicted as an old bald man with long whiskers and an extremely elongated forehead, with his additional attributes being a crane and a turtle—both symbols of longevity.

Hachiman

Hachiman, or Yahata, is a result of the mixing of Shinto and Buddhist traditions: Although initially he was believed to be an incarnation of the legendary Emperor

Ōjin (270–310), his cult was incorporated into Buddhist temples after the arrival of Buddhism in Japan.

The history surrounding Emperor Ōjin's life is a part of Japan's legendary history described in Kojiki and Nihon Shoki. He was supposed to have been birthed by Empress Jingū after she had invaded the Korean Peninsula, during which time he remained in her womb for three years. Those years might symbolize three harvests, as later, as Hachiman, Ōjin became the god of fertility (Aston, 2013).

As the deification of Emperor Ōjin, Hachiman also became the divine ancestor and patron of the Imperial Family. After the arrival of Buddhism in Japan, he joined the Buddhist pantheon as the protector of the state.

Traditionally, Emperor Ōjin was also regarded as the ancestor of a warrior clan of the Minamoto. They took him as their patron, and thus, Hachiman became revered by the samurai class. Over time, however, his cult spread to the peasantry and to other social classes—and as a result, today, Hachiman's shrines are numerous and his cult is very popular.

Haniyasu no kami

Haniyasu no kami is a term referring to two gods, Haniyasu-hiko and Haniyasu-hime, who are both deities of pottery and clay. There are conflicting accounts pertaining to their birth: One tradition says that they were born out of clay that was left after Izanagi and Izanami created the Japanese archipelago; another, that they were both out of Izanami's feces after her death (Ashkenazi, 2008).

Idaten

Idaten, also known as Skanda, is another Buddhist god, the guardian of Buddhist monks and their monasteries. He originated from the Chinese Buddhist pantheon, where he was believed to have been a virtuous king who always followed the Buddha's teachings, and was tasked to protect the temples in his stead when Buddha attained nirvana.

Inari Ōkami

Inari Ōkami is perhaps one of the most popular Shinto gods. He is a patron of numerous concepts: Fertility and agriculture on one hand and industry on the other; he also presides over rice, tea, and sake, the traditional Japanese alcoholic drink. But most importantly, he is the patron of foxes, who are important animals in Japanese tradition, often representations of spirits and divine beings, as we will see in the following chapters.

Although Inari Ōkami is often referred to as a male god, he can also be depicted in a female form, or in an androgynous one—perhaps a result of the conflation of three separate deities. The preferred gender under which Inari Ōkami is depicted varies depending on a region, or on a person's individual beliefs. All in all, Inari is a very universal deity that caters to all demographics and social groups.

Inari Ōkami's attested worship started around the 8th century, though it could have been earlier by as many as 300 years (Smyers, 1996). Since the 9th century, his worship began to spread and was closely tied to the kitsune—foxes with paranormal abilities, whom we will talk about in Chapter 6.

During the Edo Period, Inari Ōkami's worship as a god bringing luck was popular in Shinto as well as in Buddhism; however, as the attempts to separate and 'purify' both religions became stronger, there were some attempts to remove his shrines from Buddhist temples.

Today, the shrines of Inari are one of the most popular ones in Japan. The entrance to an Inari shrine would most often be marked by red torii, a traditional T-shaped gate. The offerings most often left at the shrines would include rice, sake, and sushi rolls with fried tofu.

One of the most important Inari shrines is located in Kyoto, on a mountain that got its name from the god. The Fushimi Inari Shrine sees numerous pilgrims every year. The pilgrimage usually starts at the foot of the mountain and is preceded by ritual purification with water.

Izanagi

Having mentioned the creator god at length already, let us focus on the part of the story yet untold: How Izanagi fled from Yomi and what happened later. Izanami, embarrassed by having been shamed by Izanagi, sent a number of thunder gods to chase after him as he was running away, but Izanagi managed to distract them: He disentangled a comb and a vine that were keeping his hair together and threw them at the gods. The objects turned into grapes and bamboo shoots. The gods stopped and ate them.

But the pursuit wasn't over. The gods caught up with Izanagi yet again at a mountain pass. This time, Izanagi threw peaches at them, and finally managed to repel them. This led to the god declaring the peach to be a sacred fruit and ordering it to be grown among humans, so that it may help them in their hour of need.

In the end, Izanagi blocked the entrance to Yomi with a huge rock. Izanami, furious at this, declared her intention of killing a thousand people every day to avenge her shame. Izanagi replied that he could create a thousand and more each day, to undo her destruction.

Now came the time for Izanagi to purify himself, having had so much contact with death. He washed himself in the river and that was when, according to one tradition, his previous children with Izanami finally came to this world: When he washed his left eye, the sun goddess Amaterasu came out of it; when he washed the right eye, the moon god Tsukuyomi-no-Mikoto emerged; and finally, when he washed his nose, he produced the storm god Susanoo-no-Mikoto.

Then, Izanagi decided to divide the world among his three children. The Takamagahara, the first Heaven that arose out of the chaos, was given to Amaterasu; Tsukuyomi received the night; and Susanoo was given the seas. But Susanoo wasn't happy with his gift and he kept raging and crying out, causing storms and drying up rivers, and demanding from Izanagi to be dispatched to his mother. Izanagi, furious, finally expelled him from the world.

Here, the narrative of Izanagi ends.

Jizō

Jizō, who comes from the Sanskrit tradition, was originally a Bodhisattva named Kṣitigarbha. In Japanese tradition, he is the protector of all the vulnerable, including children and expectant mothers, as well as travelers. For this reason, his statues can be found by the roadsides and close to graveyards.

Jizō also protects the souls of deceased children, including aborted and miscarried fetuses. The souls of the children are said to be delegated to endlessly construct small towers out of stones, which are repeatedly toppled by demons; Jizō is said to protect the children from the demons and to comfort them, hiding them under his cloak.

Around 1600, a tale called *The Tale of the Fuji Cave* was composed (Kimbrough, 2006); in it, the deceased children were building a stone tower, but the demons sent violent winds and flames in order to thwart them. The flames reduced the children's bodies to ash and charred bones, which were then received by Jizō, who built them back to be whole and that is how they received their eternal happiness.

Because of these legends, the statues of Jizō and his shrines are often surrounded by small piles of stones, sometimes dressed in tiny children's clothes. Those are the offerings of the bereaved parents who lost their children, hoping that Jizō would receive them and comfort them after their death.

Jurōjin

Jurōjin is another one of the Seven Lucky Gods, and another who was originally a Chinese Taoist; similarly to Fukurokuju, he might have been influenced by the Chinese god of the southern polar star. He is the God of longevity since before he became a god, he was supposed to have been a man who lived on earth for 1,500 years.

Jurōjin is often portrayed as a small, smiling old man with a staff and a fan, and is accompanied by a deer, a symbol of longevity. Paintings and statues of Jurōjin are believed to bring their owner good luck.

Kagutsuchi

Kagutsuchi is the feral child that caused the tragedy between Izanagi and Izanami: The god of fire whose birth brought Izanami's demise. His subsequent murder by Izanagi and the creation of various gods and volcanoes out of the mutilated parts of his body marked the beginning of death in the world.

Kangiten

Kangiten, or Shōten, is another Buddhist god (known as a deva), who originated in the Indian Sanskrit tradition, where he is known as Ganesha. Kangiten is a very dualistic god: On one hand, he creates obstacles for those who try to attain enlightenment; despite being a god, he is still governed by earthly desires and very quick to be angry at those who offended him. On the other hand, he can be very helpful to people who have a special connection to him and can grant even wishes which seem impossible. Overall, Kangiten's perception as he was adopted from India through China and to Japan, changed from that of an almost-demon to a god who can battle demons.

Interestingly, Kangiten's depictions aren't kept public. His image is considered to be too sacred to be seen even by his monks, with only a select few being allowed to see them after training and having performed special rituals. We know, however, the way Kangiten is portrayed: As a dual male-female person, both of them with an elephant's head, embracing, but in a non-sexual way. It is a curious image, not found anywhere outside of East Asia; it might represent the god embracing his shakti, that is, his primordial essence (Agrawala, 1978).

Because of the mysteriousness of Kangiten's image, in the Heian Period, his cult was reserved only for the imperial court and banned from private worship. As a destroyer of demons, Kangiten was invoked in rituals of subjugation; according to a legend, when a vengeful spirit of a scholar, poet, and statesman Sugawara no Michizane (845–903), who would later become the god Tenjin, was bringing storms to the land, a monk prayed to Kangiten who managed to pacify the angry ghost.

During the Edo Period, Kangiten's worship gradually spread, even though it still remained somewhat esoteric. Some attempts were made over the years to slow down this process, with some priests emphasizing Kangiten's more destructive, demonic side in order to prevent common people from treating him like a god who could grant each and every wish. But, nonetheless, the cult spread.

In one Japanese legend, Kangiten used to be an angry demon who lived under a legendary Mount Vinayaka, known as the "Elephant-headed Mountain" or the "Mountain of Obstacles" (Faure, 2015). From there, he commanded an army of demons, destroying the humans. There was only one way to tame him: The bodhisattva of compassion, Kannon, assumed a very enticing female form and came before Kangiten. The demon immediately fell in love. But she had one condition: He had to convert to Buddhism if they were to be married. He agreed, leaving behind his evilness, and she embraced him and led him toward bliss.

Konjin

Konjin is the Shinto god of metals, associated with the directions on the compass. He is closely tied to Onmyōdō, a system of Japanese science and divination based on the principles of Chinese philosophy: The working of the five elements in accordance with the belief in yin and yang, the opposing, but also interconnecting, forces.

Because encountering Konjin was believed to be a sign of bad luck—the god could be very violent and fond of hurling curses at people—a system of geomancy was developed in order to establish Konjin's position, which depended on a year, a lunar month, and season. Geomancy is a special form of divination that uses the energies of the earth in order to harmonize a person with their environment. In Chinese philosophy and religion, it is known as feng shui; in Japan, a katatagae. A special calendar was developed based on these practices, which allowed people to avoid Konjin on any given day of the year. This calendar was especially popular during the Heian Period and would be consulted when moving a house, traveling, and undertaking public works.

Kōjin

Kōjin is the god of fire and the hearth, and sometimes even, specifically, of the stove and the kitchen. He is of ambivalent nature: On one hand, a deity of destructive fire, on the other, a symbol of the subjugation of the said destruction in the family hearth. Because of that, a tablet with his depiction would be kept near the hearth—or, in a more modern household, in the kitchen.

Kōjin is said to burn away all impurity. He also watches over households and reports any evildoers to his superior, a god of a particular village, town, or city. The Shinto gods being very diligent governors of the land—

a better version of a human government—would then convene in Izumo Province, during the tenth month of the Japanese lunar calendar, when they would discuss all the human misdeeds and decide upon punishments.

Kuebiko

Kuebiko is a very folk saint: A patron of agriculture, knowledge, and folk wisdom whose form is that of a scarecrow. Kuebiko can't walk, but can talk and impart wisdom to those who ask him for advice. In the *Kojiki*, only Kuebiko knew the true name of another god, a dwarf who would later become a helper of Ōkuninushi, an important kami of whom we will speak in a bit.

Today, Kuebiko is worshiped not only as a patron of folk wisdom but also of scholarship in general.

Kukunochi

Kukunochi is the god of trees. He might have initially been a spirit of trees who lived inside them. In some versions of the myths, he was a child of Izanagi and Izanami. Today, he is evoked in a ceremony of blessing new houses.

Kuraokami

As already mentioned, Kuraokami is the dragon-god of ice who was born out of the parts of Kagutsuchi's body mixed with Izanagi's tears. He lives in the mountains and brings rain and snow to the world. Alternatively, he might be a water snake who lives in deep waters.

Kuraokami has his own shrines where he is worshiped during the dry times of the year.

Nesaku

Nesaku is a star god who, according to some versions of the myth, was created from the blood of Kagutsuchi when his father Izanagi murdered him.

Ninigi-no-Mikoto

Ninigi-no-Mikoto is very important to the foundation myth of Japan; as a grandson of Amaterasu, he was also the great-grandfather of Emperor Jimmu. He is said to have descended from Heaven to the earth, bringing treasures with him: Later, they would become the regalia of the Japanese Imperial Family. The treasures were: The legendary sword Kusanagi no Tsurugi; a mirror called Yata no Kagami; and a jewel Yasakani no Magatama. The sword was the symbol of valor, the mirror—of wisdom, and the jewel—of benevolence. The same mirror is said to have been later used to lure Amaterasu out of her cave when she hid.

The regalia are said to have been kept by the Imperial Family of Japan until 1185 when the sword was lost during a civil war, during a battle fought at sea (Turnbull, 2006). A replica was supposed to be then forged (Selinger, 2013). To this day, the presentation of the regalia is a crucial element of the ceremony of the enthronement of the new emperor. The items are kept in sealed containers and are only seen by the emperor and chosen priests during a ceremony, which is not public (Holland & Kobayashi, n.d.). Even the location of the items outside of the ceremony is not certain, and any attempts to examine their archaeological value are rejected (Holland & Kobayashi, n.d.).

But let us come back to Ninigi-no-Mikoto. After he'd been sent to bring order to the earth, he built his palace on the top of Mount Takachiho on the island of Kyushu. He also started looking for a wife. The god of the mountain where he settled presented his two daughters to him as prospective brides: Konohanasakuya-hime and Iwanaga-hime. Ninigi chose Konohanasakuya and rejected Iwanaga, for which she cursed him, taking away his immortality. And thus, the line of the gods would gradually become the line of humans, living shorter and shorter lives.

Ninigi and Konohanasakuya had three sons, the youngest of whom, Hoori, would become Jimmu's grandfather.

Ōkuninushi

Ōkuninushi is one of the most important gods in the chronicles of *Kojiki* and *Nihon Shoki*. He, along with his numerous brothers, is the son of the god of storms Susanoo, and through him, the grandson of Izanagi and Izanami. He was the original ruler of the earth before Ninigi-no-Mikoto was sent by Amaterasu to replace him.

As the ruler of the earth, Ōkuninushi resided in the Izumo Province, and his eventual subjugation might have been a symbol of the subjugation of the said province in 250 C.E. (Palmer, 2016).

There are numerous myths tied to Ōkuninushi. First of them is a famous folk story known as *The Hare of Inaba* (Antoni, 2015). It was written down in the *Kojiki* and tells a tale of a feud between the clan of hares and the clan of sharks. The conflict led to a brutal war; at last, there was only one shark and one hare left, and the hare hopped over the shark, trying to trick him. But the shark snapped at the hare and flayed him from his fur.

Enter Ōkuninushi, who was passing by the area with his brothers—they were all going to woo the princess of the region of Inaba. The hare, being in enormous pain, asked the god and his brothers for help. But the brothers were cruel and advised the hare to wash himself in the salty seawater, and later, to lay on the shore in order to dry up. Unsurprisingly, this caused the poor hare even more pain.

But when Ōkuninushi saw the hare's suffering, he gave him good advice: To wash in fresh spring water and to later roll in the pollen of cattails, which resemble fur. Thus, the hare's fur was restored. Ōkuninushi now revealed his true nature as a god to the hare and the hare blessed him in return, promising him that he would be the one to win his princess' hand.

But that is not where the story ends. Ōkuninushi won the princess, but his brothers were furious about this. They devised a plot to kill him: First, they took him to the Hoki Province and forced him, on the pain of death, to catch a wild red boar. There was only one problem: The supposed prey wasn't a boar at all, but a large rock heated up to hotness so much so that it was red, and hurled down the hill by the brothers.

Ōkuninushi burnt himself so much that he died, but his mother petitioned the gods so that they would bring him a new life. The gods relented and brought Ōkuninushi back to life, making him even stronger and more handsome.

So, the brothers devised a second plan: They tricked him into a trap. He walked onto a tree log that had been split open, but the moment he jumped into the opening, they snapped it shut, killing him a second time.

Yet again, Ōkuninushi's mother managed to restore his life, but this time, she advised him to escape to the Kii Province, on the southern shores of the Japanese archipelago. Only there he would be safe from his brothers. There, he would also be able to find his father, Susanoo, and receive counsel from him.

Ōkuninushi did as he was instructed. But before he found Susanoo, he happened upon his daughter and his half-sister, Suseribime. When he saw her, he immediately fell in love with her—something that was not to his father's liking. So, Susanoo laid four challenges on his son.

First, he invited Ōkuninushi to his palace, where he ordered him to sleep in a room full of snakes. Fortunately, Suseribime had a magical scarf that she gave to Ōkuninushi; when he wrapped himself in it, he was safe from the snake's venom.

Then, Susanoo put Ōkuninushi in a room full of centipedes and bees; but the scarf protected him from them as well.

Seeing that his challenges were no match for Ōkuninushi, Susanoo devised a different plan: He shot an arrow over a field and ordered Ōkuninushi to fetch it. But unbeknownst to him, he set the whole field on fire.

Seeing the flames rising all around him, Ōkuninushi was near despair; but suddenly, he saw a little field mouse. The animal led him quickly to a hole where he could hide and escape the fire. Later, when the flames died down, the mouse also fetched the arrow for him.

Susanoo, now seriously wanting to humiliate his son, summoned him to his palace again. There, he ordered him to comb through his hair and pick out the lice and centipedes that lived there. Ōkuninushi obediently did so, but as he was going, he also covered his father's head with a special paste prepared by Suseribime. It tangled the hair and caused Susanoo to fall asleep. When he did, Ōkuninushi tied his hair to the rafters that were keeping his palace together. Then, he stole his father's bow and arrows, as well as his koto (a stringed musical instrument), took Suseribime with him, and fled the palace.

As they were running away, Ōkuninushi accidentally brushed Susanoo's koto over tree bark. The instrument made a noise that woke his father up; as he lifted his head, the rafters to which his hair had been tied gave way and the whole palace fell down on his head. Injured and furious, but not dead, Susanoo then pursued the couple to the very borders of Yomi, the Underworld.

But as he saw that his son was constantly outrunning him, Susanoo finally had to reluctantly give him the blessing to marry Suseribime. Then, he declared him the lord of the land of the living, whom he remained up until Ninigi-no-Mikoto replaced him.

There is a number of other tales tied to Ōkuninushi. He is said to have wooed many goddesses and to have won them through his gift of poetry, but this made Suseribime very jealous. Ōkuninushi was close to leaving her, but she also persuaded him to stay with her with a song, and so, the couple was reunited.

When he was staying with Suseribime in Izumo, Ōkuninushi one day saw a tiny god sailing on the sea in a bean pod. Ōkuninushi asked the stranger his name, but he received no reply. He then tried to ask around for the man's identity, but without success—until a toad told him to ask Kuebiko, the scarecrow god of wisdom. Kuebiko told Ōkuninushi that this was Sukunabikona-no-Kami, a god of healing. Knowing his name, Ōkuninushi was able to form an alliance with the other god, who soon became his companion and close friend. From then on, they would rule the earth together.

At last, the time has come for Ōkuninushi to give up his rule. The sun goddess Amaterasu sent a number of messengers to Ōkuninushi, but all of them either didn't report back or became distracted with other matters. One of them was Ame-no-Wakahiko, the God of grain whose subsequent death and funeral we have already talked about. At last, the god of thunder, Takemikazuchi-no-Kami, was sent to Ōkuninushi and, after winning strength contests with his sons, managed to persuade Ōkuninushi to cease his control over the earth.

Omoikane

Omoikane is the god of wisdom and intelligence. The gods would often ask him for counsel—for example, when the sun goddess Amaterasu hid in a cave, it was Omoikane who came up with a solution.

Oshirasama

Oshirasama is the protective god of the home. Sometimes, he would enter a person's house, and it is believed that when it happens, men in the house cannot eat meat and only women are allowed to touch it.

Oshirasama is a half-person, half-horse.

Ōyamatsumi

Ōyamatsumi is one of the gods who were born from Kagutsuchi's mutilated body. He is the deity of mountains, sea, and war. He was also the father of Konohanasakuya-hime and Iwanaga-hime, the two young women who were offered to Ninigi-no-Mikoto in marriage. It was through Ōyamatsumi's divine power that Iwanaga-hime cursed Ninigi-no-Mikoto with a shortened lifespan after he rejected her as his bride.

Raijin

Raijin is the violent god of lightning who emerged from Izanami's body after her death. His very characteristic depiction features him as a muscular, half-naked man with a terrifying expression on his face and hair flowing in the air. His attributes are taiko drums, traditional Japanese percussion instruments—it is believed that he plays them in order to create thunder. In depictions and in worship, Raijin is often paired with his brother Fūjin.

In the most famous myth featuring Raijin, he emerged from Izanami's rotting body when she was already in Yomi. Different aspects of Raijin arose from different parts of Izanami's body, and when Izanagi saw this, he was terrified. As the god was fleeing from the Underworld, Raijin, and other demon-gods pursued him. From that point onward, Raijin would rage and cause mischief in the world.

Another story tells how Raijin was captured. He caused a massive storm, so big in fact that the emperor sent his messenger to capture him. The messenger first tried to persuade Raijin to come willingly; but when this failed and Raijin laughed in the messenger's face, he prayed to the bodhisattva of compassion, Kannon, who finally managed to capture Raijin. The god of thunder was then delivered to the emperor in a sack. The emperor promised that he would let him go, but only if from now on, he only brought rain and fertility to Japan, and not violent storms. Raijin promised and was let go; and in the future, indeed, he was less destructive, unless it was against Japan's enemies. It is said that when the Mongols invaded Japan in the 13th century, Raijin repelled them with his storms.

Ryūjin

Ryūjin is another one of the Japanese dragon-gods. He is the tutelary deity of the sea, representing the devouring nature of the ocean through his large mouth. However, over the timespan of Japanese history, the sea has been a source of life and food more often than it was a destructive force—hence, Ryūjin is considered a positive god and a patron of Japan. His storm was supposed to have drowned the Mongol fleet in the 13th century.

But Ryūjin also has the power to change into a human and, apparently, also possesses the knowledge of medicine.

There are several stories tied to Ryūjin; one of them is an origin story of how the jellyfish lost their bones. It is told that one day, Ryūjin had a very particular craving for a monkey's liver. So, he sent his servant, a jellyfish, to get him a monkey.

But the monkey was more clever than the jellyfish: When the jellyfish caught up with it, it said that it kept its liver in a special jar in the forest and had first to go and fetch it. The gullible jellyfish agreed, and thus, the monkey got away. When Ryūjin heard about this, he was so angry that he beat the jellyfish repeatedly, crushing all its bones.

Another story tells how Ryūjin was able to control the high and low tides with special jewels, called kanju and manju. The legend says that the god helped Empress Jingū in her attack on Korea, manipulating the tides with those jewels. Jingū first threw the kanju into the sea when she saw the Korean navy; it allowed the sea to recede, stranding the Korean fleet in the sand. The crew had no choice but to leave the ships; but then, the empress threw the manju, and the sea came back with double force, drowning the Koreans.

Seidai Myōjin

Seidai Myōjin is the god of sports. He is vastly popular to this day, worshiped especially in the Shiramine Shrine in Kyoto as the patron of football and kemari, the traditional Japanese version of football.

Shōtoku Taishi

Shōtoku Taishi, also known as Prince Shōtoku, was initially a semi-historical, semi-legendary figure. He was supposed to have lived between 574 and 622 C.E. and was a regent under Empress Suiko of the Asuka Period. During his time, he was a famed reformer of the administration and one of the first promoters of Buddhism. He ordered the construction of one of the first Buddhist temples, the Shitennō-ji in modern-day Osaka. He was also, famously, one of the first people to call the Japanese archipelago "the land of the rising sun," which he did in his letter to the Chinese emperor (Varley, 1977).

Over the years, a number of legends arose around Prince Shōtoku, and he eventually came to be worshiped as a god. According to one of the legends, when the sage-god Daruma came to Japan, he met Prince Shōtoku. Daruma was dressed as a beggar and refused to give his name to the prince, but Shōtoku gave him food and drink anyway. He also gifted Daruma with a purple cloak and sang as he was sleeping.

The next day, the beggar died. Shōtoku was sad and ordered his burial; but after some time, it was discovered that the man's coffin was empty and only the folded purple cloak lay inside. The prince retrieved the garment; he now knew that he had met a great sage.

Shōtoku is a very popular figure in Japan to this day, and a number of institutions have been named after him. He also appeared on coins and banknotes.

Suijin

Suijin is the god of water of a benevolent kind: He lives in rivers, streams, lakes, wells, and waterfalls. He is the guardian of the fishermen. On the other hand, through his ties to water, he is also the god of fertility, and by association, of motherhood and childbirth. He was often worshiped by people who wanted to provide fresh water and the right sanitary conditions for expectant mothers.

Suijin is worshiped in a number of shrines and during a variety of religious festivals. Most of these festivals are tied to agriculture, as it is a custom to pray to Sujin to ensure enough water for the crops, or to bring bounty to the fishermen. Expectant mothers also pray to Suijin for a safe delivery—and everyone prays to him for deliverance from drowning.

Sukunabikona

Sukunabikona is the god of hot springs, sake brewing, healing, magic, agriculture, and knowledge. He is the tiny partner and friend of Ōkuninushi who helped him build and govern the land of Japan. It is said that he invented cures for the most common illnesses, as well as protection spells, in order to help Ōkuninushi with his governing. He was especially efficient with his help against insect and snake bites.

But Sukunabikona himself wasn't impervious to illnesses. One day, he fell sick. To cure him, Ōkuninushi took him to a hot spring in Dōgo Onsen (today's city of Matsuyama). He put Sukunabikona into the spring and then fell asleep. When he awoke, his friend was completely cured and he was dancing on the stones near the spring—an act that left imprints in the stone, which are visible to this day.

Ōkuninushi and Sukunabikona's partnership ended when one day, Sukunabikona climbed the millet crop; it dipped under his weight and then rebounded, flinging him all the way to the Underworld. Ōkuninushi was very sad after the disappearance of his friend.

Sumiyoshi sanjin

The Sumiyoshi sanjin are a pair of two gods, Sokotsutsu no O no Mikoto, and Nakatsutsu no O no Mikoto— gods of the sea and sailing. They might also be a personification of the Orion stars. According to an alternative version of the legend, both gods were born when Izanagi purified himself after his visit to Yomi.

Susanoo-no-Mikoto

Finally, we come to the famous god of storms, the brother of Amaterasu and Tsukuyomi, the son of Izanagi and Izanami, and the wrathful father of Ōkuninushi. Susanoo-no-Mikoto is both a turbulent, angry god of storms and a hero who is credited with battling many monsters. There are numerous stories tied to him in Japanese chronicles and legends, and some of them we have already told, but let us complete this picture.

One version of the legend about the birth of Tsukuyomi, Amaterasu, and Susanoo said that Susanoo was immediately expelled from the earth by Izanagi due to his violent nature. Of course, he was not content with that state of affairs and tried to come back. Upon the pretext of saying one last goodbye to Amaterasu, he ascended the Takamagahara, making the heavens shake and cry out.

Amaterasu, though she was suspicious of Susanoo's intentions, agreed to meet him. Susanoo then proposed that they both participate in a ritual that would prove his good intentions: Ukehi, a trial by pledge. Each participant was supposed to chew and spit out an object brought by the other person entering the pledge.

Susanoo gave Amaterasu his sword; she broke it into three parts, chewed them, and spat them out. Three goddesses were formed from those parts. Then, she gave Susanoo her necklace which he broke into five parts, chewed, and spat out—and thus, five gods were born. Then, Amaterasu declared that the gods, since they were born out of her necklace, belonged to her, and the goddesses belonged to Susanoo.

Susanoo's good intentions were proven, and he roared in victory. Now, he could declare his true intentions: He started ravaging Amaterasu's rice fields and defiled her palace. Furious, Amaterasu fled from the heavens and hid in a cave—a start to the story we already know. For his transgressions, Susanoo was thrown from the heavens forever.

There are many stories about Susanoo and his exploits during his banishment. He killed a goddess who produced food from the orifices in her body and replenished the earth's food supply; but more importantly, he encountered Yamata no Orochi, a monstrous serpent. In Izumo province, that giant snake had devoured all seven daughters of an elderly couple whom Susanoo met on his way—and the time was coming when the eighth daughter, Kushinadahime, would also be killed and eaten.

Susanoo promised the distressed parents that he would kill the snake. To do this, he transformed himself into a comb which Kushinadahime then put in her hair. When the serpent approached, the daughter, as instructed, offered him a drink of a particularly strong sake, pretending that it was a gift. The snake guzzled it all down and fell asleep, drunk. Then Susanoo turned back into his mighty form and killed the monster.

He then proceeded to hack the serpent's body into pieces. But when he struck the tail, his sword broke. He hacked some more with a broken sword until he heard a metallic sound: A weapon was hidden in the serpent's tail. Susanoo took it out; it was a magnificent sword which Susanoo named Kusanagi no Tsurugi; later, he would use it as a reconciliatory gift when he met his sister Amaterasu again; and Amaterasu would gift the sword to Ninigi-no-Mikoto—and thus, it would become a part of the Imperial Regalia of Japan.

Having killed the serpent, Susanoo wanted to erect his palace in Izumo. He appointed Kushinadahime's father as his steward and married Kushinadahime. Later, he would also marry other women and have many children with them—one of them Ōkuninushi, though some accounts say that he was only his descendant and not his direct son. The incident with Ōkuninushi which we have already described also took place around the palace that Susanoo had erected in Izumo.

As we can see, there is much contradiction in Susanoo's image: A disruptor of peace and a troublemaker on one hand, and a noble slayer of a serpent on the other. There is some evidence to suggest that he was originally a Korean god, imported to Japan; and perhaps that is one of the reasons why his image is so ambiguous (Gadaleva, 2000).

Tajimamori

Tajimamori is a legendary hero from the Kofun Period, who lived during the reign of Emperor Suinin (ca. 29 B.C.E.–70 C.E.); but today, he is worshiped as the god of sweets.

According to the legend, Emperor Suinin ordered Tajimamori to get him a magical fruit—most likely a tachibana orange. In order to do this, the hero set out on a ten-year-long journey, but when he returned with the fruit, the emperor was already dead. Tajimamori gave half of the fruit to his widow; the other half he put on the emperor's grave. Then, he sat by the grave and cried in sadness; soon, he died there out of grief.

After his death, Tajimamori became associated with the fruit he carried and, by association, also with sweets.

Today, he is worshiped by the confectioners and producers of sweets.

Takemikazuchi

Takemikazuchi is the god of thunder, one of the gods who emerged from Kagutsuchi's body. He would often be sent by the gods from heaven to the earth in order to subdue the earthly gods, among them Ōkuninushi. Takemikazuchi battled and subdued his sons, which forced Ōkuninushi to relinquish his control. His combat with Takeminakata, in which he crushed his hand, became the first ever known instance of sumo wrestling.

Years later, when Emperor Jimmu was conquering Japan, an old man came to him with a mighty sword. When Jimmu asked him what the weapon was, he said that he had had a dream in which the gods wanted to send Takemikazuchi to subdue the earth yet again. But the god of thunder said that this time, only his sword in Jimmu's hand would be sufficient to conquer Japan. And indeed, the sword instantly cut all of Jimmu's enemies.

Takeminakata

Takeminakata, the god who fought with Takemikazuchi, is the deity of wind, water, hunting, warfare, and agriculture. Historically, he was especially worshiped by the samurai. He was believed to have been an ancestor of the Suwa clan and is now worshiped in the Suwa Grand Shrine next to Lake Suwa in Nagano Prefecture.

Takeminakata's defeat by Takemikazuchi is depicted as rather shameful in *Kojiki* (Philippi, 1968). There, Takeminakata begged for his life after Takemikazuchi crushed his arm. But in other versions of the myth, it was portrayed as more of a noble defeat; in those versions, Takeminakata was thrown to the ground, as it befitted a first-ever sumo wrestling (von Krenner, 2013).

After his defeat by Takemikazuchi, Takeminakata traveled the land, where he had a number of adventures, most of which involved fighting with divine opponents in a similar style as he did with the messenger from heaven. Most notably, he defeated Moriya, a local god from the Suwa Prefecture. For that, he was besieged by Moriya's compatriots, but some of the people from Suwa swore allegiance to him. Thus, he became the first king of the Suwa and the ancestor of the Suwa clan.

Later, as the king of Suwa, Takeminakata was often portrayed as a god who had the ability to turn into a water serpent.

Tamanoya

Tamanoya is the god of jewelry, most specifically, of the Magatama beads from the Kofun Period. These were tear- or comma-shaped beads made of jade, very characteristic of the era. In the myth about Amaterasu and Susanoo exchanging gifts as a part of their pledge, Amaterasu's necklace was made of Magatama beads.

Ta-no-Kami

Ta-no-Kami is primarily the god of the farmers, as he is believed to preside over the rice harvest. He is worshiped mainly in spring and autumn when the rice is subsequently planted and harvested. Although there are different ceremonies depending on the region, most of them feature dances and eating rice cakes.

Similarly to Kuebiko, a scarecrow is often believed to be Ta-no-Kami's representation. In this form, he repeals the spirits of violent animals and birds from the fields.

Tenjin

Tenjin, the god of scholars and learning, is another example of a historical figure who became deified. Contrary to most of them, however, the earthly form of Tenjin—the politician, scholar, and poet Sugawara no Michizane (845–903)—wasn't only a legendary figure, but definitely a historical one.

As a politician, Sugawara was a governor of the Sanuki Province who came into conflict with the powerful Fujiwara clan, which ultimately led to his banishment and death in exile. As a poet, he was renowned for his works both in Chinese and Japanese.

However, Tenjin's first emergence as a god wasn't tied to his poetry and scholarship. In 930, 17 years after Sugawara's death in exile, Kyoto was struck by a series of lightning and heavy rain, as well as a plague. During these events, many members of the Fujiwara clan died and their houses were destroyed; soon, this was interpreted as a sign that Sugawara's angry spirit was enacting revenge from behind the grave. To pacify him, Sugawara's titles and offices were posthumously destroyed and the edict of his banishment was burned; furthermore, a cult of Tenjin, "the Sky Deity," was established (Pawasarat, 2020).

Over the years, however, Tenjin was less remembered for his anger and more for the poetry he composed during his lifetime. During the Edo Period, his works were widely commented on and renowned, and slowly, his cult morphed from that of a deity of the elements, and more into a deity of learning.

Tenjin is still very popular today: Many Japanese students pray to him before their exams and thank him later if the result is favorable. His role as an angry god has been completely eclipsed by his intelligence.

Tsukuyomi-no-Mikoto

As we have mentioned many times, Tsukuyomi-no-Mikoto was one of the original triads of gods birthed by Izanagi and Izanami. Tsukuyomi is the god of the Moon, and unlike his siblings Amaterasu and Susanoo, he mostly didn't engage in conflicts over the domination of the world. However, there was one instance in which he angered his sister.

One day, Amaterasu sent Tsukuyomi to represent her at a feast thrown by Ukemochi, the goddess of food. But when Tsukuyomi saw the way in which she produced food, he was disgusted. She created fish by spitting into the ocean; game, by spitting into the forest; and a rice paddy, by coughing into a rice bowl. In his disgust, Tsukuyomi killed her.

Soon, Amaterasu found out what happened. She was so angry at her brother that she moved into an entirely different part of the sky, refusing to ever see him again. And thus, their subsequent roles as heavenly bodies were established: Amaterasu as the Sun, and Tsukuyomi as the Moon.

Yakushi Nyorai

The final god on our list is, yet again, a Buddhist deity. Yakushi Nyorai is the Buddha of medicine who has the power of eliminating afflictions by entering the state of the so-called samadhi, or, meditative consciousness. In Japan, he was one of the important Wisdom Buddhas and, even though over the centuries, some of his importance was transferred onto Jizō, he is still invoked in funerary rites.

Yakushi Nyorai is often portrayed surrounded by the so-called Twelve Heavenly Generals, who are his protective minor deities.

Chapter 4:

Goddesses

The list of Japanese goddesses, even though shorter than that of the gods, is still an extensive one. Let us now talk about them and their fascinating world.

Amanozako

Amanozako, in a way, is Susanoo's daughter—he spit her out when his angry spirit built up inside him. As a result, Amanozako is monstrous: She has long ears and a long nose, as well as fangs that can chew even metal; she can also fly.

There is really no single area of expertise that Amanozako occupies herself with. In a way, she is a trickster goddess—she always acts against social norms and displays unquenchable anger.

Amaterasu-Ōmikami

Amaterasu, the sun goddess whom we have already met many times, is probably the most important goddess in the Japanese pantheon. She is the ruler of the whole of Takamagahara and the primary ancestress of the Imperial House of Japan.

We have already told the most important myths about Amaterasu: About her birth; her conflict with Susanoo and her subsequent hideout in a cave; and how she was lured out of it. We also know about her conflict with her other brother, Tsukuyomi, and how she was sending messengers to the earth to put it under the jurisdiction of her descendant, Ninigi. She then gave Ninigi three of the treasures that would later become the sacred treasures of the Imperial House of Japan: The sword that Susanoo gave her after he slew the serpent; and the mirror and the jewel that were used to lure her out of her cave.

There are a number of stories involving Amaterasu that originate from various times during the reign of different emperors. Many of them tell origin stories behind various shrines dedicated to the goddess, the most famous of them being the one in Ise in Mie Prefecture. One myth tells a story of how the legendary Empress Jingū was possessed by various gods, including

Amaterasu, who told her about a rich land over the sea, which, in the end, prompted her invasion of Korea.

Over the years, the cult of Amaterasu became very important, sometimes even to the point of neglect of other kami—a veritable cult of the sun (Wheeler, 2013).

Ame-no-Uzume

Ame-no-Uzume is the goddess of the dawn, but also of joy, art, meditation, and revelry. This combination might seem incongruous, but let us not forget that it was Ame-no-Uzume's trance-induced dance and taking off her clothes that prompted the gods to laugh and, in turn, intrigued Amaterasu so much that she peeked out of the cave in which she had been hiding.

Later, when Ninigi was sent to the earth by Amaterasu, Ame-no-Uzume was ordered to accompany him. However, as they were dismounting from the sky, a lesser deity, Sarutahiko Ōkami who, at the time, was the leader of the earthly gods, blocked their path. Ame-no-Uzume, who was very clever, decided to use her female charms to flirt with Sarutahiko, who, as he became distracted, let Ninigi pass.

It is said that later, Ame-no-Uzume fell genuinely in love with Sarutahiko. They married and were the ancestors of one of the prominent Japanese clans, the Sarume clan.

Benzaiten

Benzaiten was originally a Hindu goddess who was adopted by the Japanese through Chinese culture around the 6th century. She is the goddess of learning, arts, and speech. She is one of the Seven Lucky Gods and is believed to give money to those who pray to her.

Benzaiten is often depicted with eight arms that hold different objects: A sword and a Japanese lute, and sometimes a special jewel that grants wishes.

Izanami

We already know so much about Izanami, her act of creation of the Japanese archipelago and of the primary Shinto gods, as well as her death and the events that transpired in the Underworld. But do we know what happened to Izanami later?

She was trapped in Yomi as Izanagi ran away from there and blocked the entrance with a large boulder. It seems that from now on, the previously loving couple of creator gods would be in perpetual conflict: Izanami vowed that she would kill a thousand of the inhabitants of the earth every day, to which Izanagi replied that he would bring to life 1,500 people every day to make up for that. From then on, that duality between life and death would define Izanami and Izanagi.

Kannon

Kanoon was originally Guanyin, the Chinese-Buddhist bodhisattva of compassion. In China, she was initially depicted as a man, but in Japan, she is predominantly female. We have already met her on a couple of occasions: When she enticed Kangiten with her beauty and captured Raijin. But apart from her association with compassion and taming that which is violent, she is also regarded in Japan as a protector of travelers—and in the modern world, she is believed to prevent cars from accidents. Because of her gentle nature, she is also associated with vegetarianism.

There are many local versions of Kannon. She is worshiped as a protector of the elderly and mothers going through childbirth and raising young children. When the first Christian missionaries arrived in Japan and tried to convert the Japanese people, they often compared Kannon to the Virgin Mary.

Kaya-no-hime

Kaya-no-hime is the goddess of grass and fields and, more broadly speaking, vegetation. She is the wife of Ōyamatsumi, the god of sea and mountains, and according to some, one of the many children of Izanagi and Izanami whom they had before the most important triad. Kaya-no-hime is also the mother of Konohanasakuya-hime, the goddess of Mount Fuji, whom we will talk about in a bit.

People often pray to Kaya-no-hime before cutting down trees as a building material, so that they could create a sturdy home. She is also regarded as the inventor of herbs, and so, their beneficiary properties are regarded as her work.

Kisshōten

Kisshōten, also known as Kichijōten, was originally a Hindu Buddhist goddess. She would sometimes be worshiped as one of the Seven Lucky Gods; however, there are variants of this group of deities where she is not listed. Her specialty is beauty and happiness, as well as fertility.

Konohanasakuya-hime

Konohanasakuya-hime is a special goddess: The deity of Mount Fuji, as well as all volcanoes, who is said to be surrounded by cherry blossoms. Because of this combination of the most iconic elements of Japan, she is often considered a literal embodiment of Japanese life. It is worth noting that, unlike many male gods associated with fire, storms, or volcanoes, Konohanasakuya-hime is gentle and prevents the volcanoes from erupting, rather than causing them to.

There are a couple of legends tied to Konohanasakuya-hime. She was the chosen bride of Ninigi-no-Mikoto, for which her sister, Iwanaga, cursed him with taking away his immortality.

But that wasn't the end of the problems. After only one night with Ninigi, Konohanasakuya-hime became pregnant—something that made Ninigi suspicious. The goddess was so angered by her husband's accusation that she shut herself in a hut without doors or windows. Then, she set the hut on fire—after all, she was the volcano goddess, and if her child was truly to be hers and Ninigi's, it wouldn't be harmed.

And that is what happened: Inside the hut, Konohanasakuya-hime gave birth to three sons: Hoderi,

Hosuseri, and Hoori. Hoori, the youngest, would later become the grandfather of Emperor Jimmu.

There is another legend about Konohanasakuya-hime, which was written in the 11th century (*Ancient tales*, n.d.). In this tale, a boy named Yosoji lived in a village that had been struck by a smallpox plague; and one day, Yosoji's mother fell ill, too. So, the boy went to a fortune-teller, who told him to gather water near Mount Fuji and give it to his mother.

The next day, Yosoji went on a trek. But when he was nearing the mountain, he came to a crossroads. There were three possible paths, and he didn't know which one of them to take.

Suddenly, a young girl clad in a white robe appeared before him. She said that she knew the area, and guided him to a stream. Yosoji gathered some water for his mother; but he wanted to cure his neighbors and the whole village, too.

The girl told him that she would meet him at the crossroads in three days' time. It would take five more trips for the water to cure the village, she said. With this promise, she left Yosoji, and he came back to his mother and gave her water to drink.

And the girl's word was true: Five trips later, the whole village, including Yosoji's mother, was cured. The villagers thanked the boy profusely, but he refused to accept gratitude; it was all thanks to the girl. So, he went to hike up Mount Fuji one more time, in hopes of finding the girl and thanking her.

But when he came to the now well-known spot where the stream had been flowing, he found the place completely dried up. The girl was nowhere to be seen, either.

Yosoji started praying. He wished for the girl to reveal her name to him so that he would know whom to thank. And then, the woman appeared before him one last time; she said that her name wasn't important. But she had camellia flowers in her hair, and when she turned away, a cloud descended from the top of Mount Fuji and picked her up. Then, Yosoji finally realized: The girl was Konohanasakuya-hime herself.

Kushinadahime

Kushinadahime was the woman whom Susanoo-no-Mikoto rescued from the terrible serpent and later married. Today, she is mostly worshiped alongside her husband in multiple shrines throughout Japan.

Tamayori-hime

Tamayori-hime is the mother of Emperor Jimmu. She is the daughter of Watatsumi, the water dragon who emerged from Kagutsuchi's severed body. She met Ugayafukiaezu—Jimmu's future father—when he was still a little child and she was sent to care for him by her sister, Toyotama-hime, who was the child's mother but had abandoned the child. As Ugayafukiaezu grew up, he started to love his aunt and eventually, they were married. Not much more is known about Tamayori-hime from that point.

Toyotama-hime

Toyotama-hime, the grandmother of Emperor Jimmu and sister of Tamayori-hime, was much more tied to the sea—the domain of her father, Watatsumi—than her sister. After she gave birth to Ugayafukiezu, she immediately returned to the sea, leaving the child on the seashore and in the care of her sister.

But how did it happen that she gave birth in the first place? Toyotama-hime had lived with her father in his palace made of fish scales, at the bottom of the sea.

But one day, a young prince—Hoori—came to the seashore in search of a fishing hook he had lost. The hook had been borrowed from his older brother, Umisachi, and Hoori was scared that he would be very angry if he learned about the loss.

At the same time, Toyotama-hime came to the shore; she needed fresh water from a nearby well. Hoori came up to her and asked for a drink. Captivated by his beauty, Toyotama-hime offered it to him; she later related the whole affair to her father.

Watatsumi recognized that Hoori was a prince from a renowned house; so he invited him to dine at his underwater palace, where he and Toyotama-hime were soon married. They lived happily together for three years.

But then, Hoori revealed that he still had unfinished business to attend to the matter of Umisachi's hook. As it happened, the hook had caught in the throat of one of the fish at the palace. Hoori retrieved it and was sent to the surface with some advice from his wife and father-in-law. This allowed him not only to return the hook to his brother but also to overpower him.

Then, Toyotama, who returned to the surface with her husband, announced that she was pregnant. Hoori built her a special house for safe delivery which was made of cormorant feathers.

Toyotama then went into labor. She had only one condition for the safe delivery: Hoori couldn't watch her as she gave birth. He complied and waited outside of the house.

But unfortunately, as it's often the case with these things, Hoori couldn't rein in his curiosity, and he peeked inside. But to his horror, he didn't see his wife in the hut: Instead, a giant crocodile was nursing the baby. Hoori cried out in anguish, and the crocodile looked up: It was, of course, still Toyotama-hime—a true daughter of her dragon father—who had shapeshifted to give birth.

Ashamed of having been seen in her monstrous form, Toyotama-hime immediately returned to the sea, leaving the child in the hut. Soon after, she sent her sister, Tamayori-hime, to care for it. We know the rest of the story.

Toyouke-Ōmikami

Toyouke-Ōmikami is the goddess of agriculture on one hand, and of industry on the other. The legend says that originally, she had been worshiped in the Tanba Province. But one day, during the reign of one of the legendary Japanese emperors, Yūryaku (418–479), the emperor had an unsettling dream. Amaterasu herself came to him and said that she couldn't supply enough food for the people in Japan; but there was a goddess who could, for she was responsible for the meals of the gods. It was Toyouke-Ōmikami, and the emperor had to bring her over from Tanba.

So the emperor built a place of worship for Toyouke-Ōmikami in Amaterasu's Ise Grand Shrine; the famine was averted, and from then on, Toyouke-Ōmikami became Amaterasu's food supplier.

There is another legend tied to the goddess, from before she was called from Tanba. It is said that one day, Toyouke-Ōmikami was bathing in a spring and left her cloak on the shore. An elderly couple saw it and took it, rendering the goddess unable to return to the heavens. The couple then used the robe to bind the goddess to themselves and force her to enchant their homemade sake so that it cured every illness.

But after ten years of this, the couple threw the goddess away from their home, and she was forced to wander aimlessly through the earth—until she was called upon her new mission.

Ugajin

Ugajin is the deity of the harvest who can take both male and female forms. In the feminine version, she is depicted with the body of a coiled snake and the head of a woman. Sometimes, she would be fused with the Buddhist goddess of learning, Benzaiten—a snake representing the aquatic aspect of the goddess. Thus, Ugajin would sometimes be treated as Benzaiten's essence.

Ukemochi

We have already mentioned Ukemochi—the goddess of food whose way of producing nourishment by spitting it out offended Tsukuyomi-no-Mikoto so much. But another version of this story is that Ukemochi's encounter was not with Tsukuyomi, but with Susanoo, who asked her for food, which she produced out of her mouth, nose, and rectum. Disgusted—and also suspecting that Ukemochi had poisoned the food—Susanoo killed her. From her body, silkworms crawled out, and various crops grew out of various parts of her body: Rice, millet, wheat, and soybeans. Thus, the most popular crops grown in Japan were born.

Wakahiru-me

Wakahiru-me is the goddess of the rising sun. She is the daughter of Amaterasu, and can be sometimes interpreted as an aspect of her, specifically, of the sun rising in the morning.

Wakahiru-me is also the divine weaver: She makes garments for the gods. There is one fragmentary legend that says that the perpetual troublemaker, Susanoo, once threw a flaming pony at the heavens and killed Wakahiru-me who was sitting at her loom and spinning (Turner & Coulter, 2001).

Wakahiru-me closes our overview of goddesses in the Japanese tradition. In the next chapter, we will talk about heroes: Some of them human, some semi-divine, and most of them interacting with the gods.

Chapter 5:

Heroes

We are now slowly descending from the immortal plane in order to meet some human heroes from Japanese myth and folklore. But we will not leave the gods and goddesses entirely behind: Our protagonists, whether brave princesses, unassuming heroes, or extraordinary children, will interact with gods, spirits, and other creatures more often than not. Let us now learn their stories.

Hachikazuki

Our first heroine is a princess. The tale of Hachikazuki was first recorded between the 14th and 16th centuries and tells a story of a young girl who finds her love (Seiki, 1966).

An elderly couple had a beautiful daughter, whom they loved dearly, but also guarded against any possible wrongdoers.

One day, the elderly mother of the girl fell ill. Soon, she was on her deathbed; her time had come. As her last wish, she made Hachikazuki swear that she would wear a wooden bowl on her head at all times, in order to cover her otherworldly beautiful face. The girl swore to do so.

After the mother's death, the father remarried. The stepmother didn't care much about Hachikazuki; in fact, she was so cruel that the girl had to escape the house and travel to a different city, where she hired herself as a servant in a noble household.

She served there for a while until the son of her master spotted her one day as she was bathing. In order to wash her face, Hachikazuki took the bowl briefly off her face. The young nobleman perceived the beauty of the girl and immediately fell in love with her. When there came a time for him to choose a wife, he insisted that Hachikazuki would be listed among the candidates.

And, in the end, everything ended happily: The young nobleman chose Hachikazuki and immediately, the bowl cracked into pieces and fell off her head. It not only revealed her beauty to the world but, as it also turned out, it contained a plethora of gems that the girl now possessed as her dowry. Her noble origin was also revealed. The couple married and, presumably, lived happily ever after.

The story of Hachikazuki is a Japanese example of a Cinderella-type story—a type of tale that could be found all around the world. But when it comes to Japan's immediate surroundings, this type of tale, albeit in a slightly different variant, was recorded in China in the 9th century (Beauchamp, 2010).

Issun-Bōshi

Issun-Bōshi literally means "One-Sun Boy," but is often translated as "The Inch-High Samurai," since *sun* in this context refers to the Japanese measurement unit, around 3 centimeters. It's a story about the most unassuming of heroes, but probably, given his size, the bravest one. It was written between the 14th and 16th centuries.

Yet again, this story starts with an elderly couple. They couldn't have children, so they prayed to the three Sumiyoshi sanjin gods. The deities heard their prayer, but the child who was born never grew taller than one *sun*.

Nevertheless, the couple loved the boy dearly. They named him Issun-Bōshi on account of his height and gave him everything he needed.

But the boy had one dream: He wanted to become a samurai. From the moment he was born, he'd heard stories about brave warriors who lived by the samurai code. And Issun-Bōshi was brave; after all, he had to be brave, living in a world that, from his perspective, had been made for giants.

So one day, Issun-Bōshi decided to go to the capital. He prepared his journey well; he fashioned a boat out of a rice bowl and a paddle out of a chopstick. He even prepared his weapon: A needle became his sword, and a straw his scabbard. Thus equipped, he set out on his journey.

In the capital, he found employment in a nobleman's household. However, he still felt like the family dismissed him, treating him only like a small child. But soon, he would find a way to prove himself.

The family whom Issun-Bōshi was serving had a young daughter. One day, as the girl was walking to a palace, she got kidnapped by an oni—an ogre-like demon. Issun-Bōshi, who was accompanying her on her journey as an escort, tried to fight the oni back, but he got swallowed by him in the process.

Fortunately, Issun-Bōshi didn't lose his needle-sword. Inside He started stabbing the oni from the inside— making life unbearable for the demon because of the constant pricking. At last, the oni had to spit Issun-Bōshi out. He was, in fact, so fed up with Issun-Bōshi that he fled to the mountains, leaving the girl behind.

He also left a magic hammer. It had the power of granting its owner wishes if they tapped it on the ground. Now, Issun-Bōshi, who had been in love with the girl whom he was serving, but was unable to pursue his feelings because of his height, wished to grow to an average human height. When his wish was granted, the brave samurai married the girl, with the blessing of her family who were amazed at his bravery. And thus, they lived happily ever after.

Kintarō

The story of Kintarō is the most traditional tale of a brave hero with supernatural strength who battled monsters. His road to glory wasn't easy, however.

Kintarō was born to a princess named Yaegiri. Unfortunately, during that time, her husband, a samurai by the name of Sakata, was engaged in a feud with his uncle, a very powerful and dangerous man. Afraid for her child's life, the princess had to flee and leave the child in the wilderness surrounding Mount Ashigara.

There, the child was picked up by a yama-uba, a type of spirit that could probably best be translated as a mountain witch. The witch decided to raise the little boy who, from the very start, showed signs of restlessness and great strength.

As Kintarō grew up, he was getting stronger and stronger. Soon, he would be able to uproot trees with his bare hands and crush rocks in his fists. He was plump and of a ruddy complexion, and he never grew cold, only wearing a short bib with a Japanese character for 'gold' embroidered on it; that is how he became known as Kintarō, "the Golden Boy."

From a very early age, Kintarō befriended animals—there were no children to grow up with on the mountain slopes—and even learned their language. Soon, the wild beasts of the forest became his companions and mounts. He wrestled bears like a real sumo and, with the help of his animal friends, defeated monsters and demons. He would also be helpful to humans, assisting them with cutting trees.

When Kintarō grew up, he was spotted in the forest by the leader of the powerful Fujiwara clan by the name of Minamoto no Yorimitsu (948–1021). The samurai and lord were so impressed by Kintarō's strength that he immediately beckoned him to come to Kyoto with him and to become his retainer. In Kyoto, after some strenuous training, Kintarō became a member of

Minamoto's special guard, also known as Shitennō—a group of four retainers of special qualities.

In Kyoto, Kintarō lived a long and prosperous life, having found his birth mother and brought her to live with him. Here, the old story ends; but Kintarō lives on even today, as he is an exceptionally popular folk hero, with numerous books, manga, anime, and even action figures dedicated to him. Dolls representing Kintarō are often gifted to mothers who have given birth to baby boys; the tradition is that the possession of such a doll will help the boy become as courageous and strong as Kintarō himself. There are also shrines dedicated to his worship.

Kiyohime

The story of Kiyohime is a tale of a woman whose love was scorned, and about the disastrous consequences. The earliest versions of the story come from the 11th and 12th centuries, subsequently (Szostak, 2013).

Our tale starts with a young Buddhist monk who was traveling south on a pilgrimage from his homeland in the area of modern-day Fukushima. On his way there, he took up an offer from a steward of a vast manor house and decided to lodge there for a night.

The steward had a daughter, the beautiful Kiyohime. When she saw the monk, she immediately fell in love with him. Knowing that he will soon be gone, she decided to act quickly and confessed her feelings. But the monk, who did not return them, also lacked integrity and honesty to speak truthfully about his lack of affection; instead, he promised Kiyohime that he would return to her after his pilgrimage—only to get rid of her advances.

But Kiyohime wasn't stupid. She realized that the monk was, in reality, rejecting her, and as soon as he set off, she pursued him, filled with rage. The monk hurried along the way until he came to a river. He bought off the ferryman, instructing him to transport him across the river, but to refuse such transport to a girl who was closing on him.

The ferryman did as instructed. Now, angered even more, Kiyohime jumped into the river and swam to the other shore; but while she was in the water, her rage transformed her into a vicious serpent.

When the monk saw his pursuer in her new monstrous form, he ran as quickly as he could to the nearest temple and asked the monks who resided there to hide him. They complied, telling him to hide under a bonshō bell—a conical bell—the kind which are very common in Buddhist temples.

But Kiyohime, in her serpent form, now had heightened senses. When she slithered into the temple, she smelt the monk hiding under the bell and coiled around it. She banged the bell several times with her tail, causing it to vibrate, and then roared fire from her mouth. The bell started melting, and the monk died in agony inside.

The story of Kiyohime is not only that of a dangerous woman scorned; but also of the danger of giving false promises.

Momotarō

The story of Momotarō is yet another one of those stories about boy heroes. Momotarō's name means "the Peach Boy," as he was born from a peach; his story was written down in the Edo Period, though it probably existed in the oral form earlier than that (Kahara, 2004).

As usual in these stories, it starts with an old childless woman. One day, she was washing her clothes by the river, when she saw a giant peach floating on the water. She caught the peach immediately—she was poor and needed to find sustenance where she could—and brought it back home to her husband.

But when the couple opened the peach in order to eat it, they discovered a little boy inside. The boy was a small child, but he was already articulate: He said that it was the gods who decided for him to become their son. The couple rejoiced and named the boy Momotarō.

Very quickly, it turned out that the boy had supernatural strength. When he was only five, he was capable of cutting trees down with his knife; and when he became a teenager, he heard of a band of demons—oni—who terrorized the area. So, of course, Momotarō decided to seek them out and defeat them.

Momotarō's journey was long. On his way, he met several supernatural creatures: A talking dog, a monkey, and a pheasant. They all agreed to help him on his quest if he fed them along the way.

Finally, Momotarō found the place where the oni dwelled: The island of demons, Onigashima. The boy's animal friends helped him infiltrate the fortress made by the demons, and he barged inside, beating the oni until they submitted to him. In the end, he captured the chief of the demons, named Ozaki, and returned home with loads of treasure and his new animal friends in tow.

This is where the story of Momotarō ends—but by no means the end of his popularity as a character. Over the years, especially at the beginning of the 20th century, the figure of Momotarō was incorporated into Japanese school curriculum, aimed at teaching children bravery, how to care for their parents, and how to battle threats. The tale of the boy was used for patriotic purposes, with Momotarō being often made into a military commander who punished the oni for their wrongdoings (Kahara, 2004). However, that usage of the tale was also criticized, as the metaphorical reading of the story suggested strongly that all foreigners should be treated like the demons were treated in the tale (Kahara, 2004). Momotarō was also used as an icon for war propaganda during World War II (Antoni, 1991). After the war, however, the perception shifted and the highly simplified version of the tale was no longer taught in schools.

Urashima Tarō

Urashima Tarō was a simple fisherman who was rewarded for his kindness. His story was recorded relatively early—around the 8th century (Holmes, 2014).

One day, Urashima Tarō was walking by the seashore, coming back from a day of hard work. Suddenly, he spotted a group of children; they were all gathered around a small turtle, torturing and taunting it. Urashima Tarō, since he was a kind man, decided to interfere; he scolded the children for their cruel behavior and released the turtle back into the sea.

The next day, as he was making his usual walk back home, Urashima Tarō met a turtle again, but this time, a far bigger one. The turtle said that the smaller kinsman whom the fisherman had saved the day before was no other than Otohime, the daughter of Ryūjin, the dragon-god of the sea. Now, she wanted to thank him for his kindness; and so, he was invited into the palace below the sea. The giant turtle gave Urashima Tarō magical gills so that he could breathe underwater—and off they went.

And so, Urashima Tarō saw the wondrous palace of Ryūgū-jō, the Palace of the Dragon God, where he met Ryūjin himself, as well as his daughter, who was now a beautiful princess in a human form. Urashima Tarō was given a tour of the palace and admired its wonders: On each side, it overlooked a different season of the year, and it was enormous. Urashima Tarō agreed to stay in the palace for three days; but later, he wanted to come back to the surface, as he had an aging mother whom he needed to take care of.

Otohime was unhappy about the fisherman's departure, but she said that she understood, and she gave him a parting gift: A magical box, called tamatebako, which was supposed to protect him from all harm, but which he was supposed never to open. Thus equipped, Urashima Tarō was brought back to the surface.

But he was so astonished when he walked onto the shore and didn't recognize his surroundings! A larger city now stood on the seashore, his old home was nowhere to be seen, and none of the people he met were his neighbors. He tried asking around for his mother, but nobody had heard about her; at last, he asked if anyone knew a man by the name of Urashima Tarō.

That is when he learned the terrible truth: 300 years had passed since he had been taken to the underwater palace. Urashima Tarō was now a name of a legend—a man who one day vanished from the seashore, never to be seen again.

Crushed by the weight of his discovery, Urashima Tarō wept on the seashore. He took out the box he had received from the princess: It was supposed to protect him from harm, but what did he care about harm now? All of his friends and family were gone; his life had been uprooted.

He opened the box.

A cloud of white smoke emerged from the inside; in a flash, Urashima felt himself aging rapidly, all the years he spent underwater catching up with him. He wrinkled and sagged, and a long white beard grew from his chin. A cry came from the sea; it was the cry of the divine princess. Very soon, Urashima died of old age.

The story of Urashima Tarō is perhaps the most heartbreaking tale of the ones we have told so far: A story of a man who was supposed to have been rewarded for his kindness, but whose mortal idea of a reward clashed with that of immortal gods. In the end, what is the difference between a reward and a punishment for those whose lives last forever?

Uriko-hime

The tale of Uriko-hime is slightly similar to that of Momotarō, in that it tells a story of a girl born out of a melon fruit. The tale has circulated in an oral version for centuries, and there are more than 100 versions of it all over the Japanese archipelago (Immos & Ikeda, 1973).

But this is what most of the versions agree on: The melon from which Uriko-hime was born was found in a river by an elderly couple, much as it was in the case of Momotarō. And in this case, the couple was overjoyed by the discovery and decided to raise the little girl, who soon became a beautiful young woman.

One day, Uriko-hime's parents had to leave the house after some errands. They left the girl cooking dinner for them but warned her not to open the door for any strangers. Uriko-hime complied and came back to her cooking.

Unfortunately, a yokai—a type of demon—saw the parents leave and the girl being left alone. The yokai's name was Amanojaku and it was known as a particularly vicious demon who could devour souls and prompt people to do wicked deeds.

When Amanojaku saw that the girl was alone, it appeared behind the front door and started calling to her. It beckoned her to open the door only a crack, and no harm would come to her. Unfortunately, Uriko-hime was slightly naive, so she agreed to the demon's plea. She opened the door, but couldn't close it again; Amanojaku forced itself inside the house. Then, it devoured the poor girl and flayed the skin from her body. The demon put the skin on and when the elderly couple came back home, it impersonated Uriko-hime to perfection.

This went on for several days. The couple didn't recognize the change, except that the girl seemed slightly moodier than before; the yokai also wrought mischief in the house whenever given the chance.

But fortunately, one day, a bird sat on the roof and started singing beautifully. This was the real Uriko-hime, reincarnated. As she sang, her parents realized that they could understand the bird's song. With horror, they discovered the truth. The story is vague on what happened later, but presumably, Amanojaku was expelled from the house.

The story of Uriko-hime closes our overview of heroes from Japanese myth, but this is by no means the end of folklore stories from this tradition. In the next chapter, we will learn some more about supernatural creatures such as the already mentioned oni and yokai; and in the last chapter, some more folktales will await your attention.

Chapter 6:

Supernatural Creatures

Japanese mythology and folklore abound not only in numerous gods and goddesses but also in supernatural creatures. Broadly speaking, there are several categories under which those creatures—spirits, demons, shapeshifters—can fall; but as we will see, not all of them are very easily classifiable. But all of them live very close to us and can interact with us almost at every turn in our lives. Below is the selection of the most important or interesting creatures.

The Obake

Most broadly speaking, the obake are shapeshifters: Special types of spirits that can change their form. In their natural form, they would often be animals, such as foxes or raccoons, or even everyday objects; but they can either transform into spirits or gain supernatural qualities in their primary forms. Let us see what types of creatures are considered obake in Japan.

Bakeneko

The bakeneko are supernatural cats. They look like ordinary cats, except for a couple of small differences: Their pupils change shape and color depending on the time of the day, and when petted, their fur produces sparks. The bakeneko are very stealthy and quiet, and they have a rather ferocious nature, even if to the naked eye they seem very docile and gentle.

At first glance, that description seems to at least partly apply to most ordinary cats; but the bakeneko are almost always old—over seven years, or, in some regional versions, over twelve or thirteen. Sometimes, they are spirits of cats who had been brutally killed by humans, and reincarnated into a new cat, only to enact revenge. For these means, they can even shapeshift into a human or possess a human.

The bakeneko have peculiar tastes: They could lick blood or lamp oil. The latter especially was often treated as a sign of a strange event to come. One possible explanation behind that odd behavior is that during the Edo Period, lamp oil was often made with various fish oils, which could attract cats.

There are many legends concerning the bakeneko from various regions (and time periods) in Japan. The oldest ones center around temples, as cats were often kept by the monks in order to protect the sacred texts from being eaten by rats. It was a belief that those cats could transform into spirits.

One more elaborate story concerning the bakeneko is of a man named Takasu Genbei, who had a pet cat that one day went missing. Very soon after this happened, Takasu's mother started behaving very oddly: She refused to socialize with people and would shut herself in her room.

One day, Takasu and other members of his family decided to check in on his mother; so they peeked inside her bedroom. But instead of a well-known middle-aged woman, they saw a giant cat wearing her clothes and munching on dead rodents.

Takasu burst into the room. Quickly, he killed the giant cat, and in a moment, its carcass turned back into an ordinary small cat—Takasu's pet that had gone missing. And when the family tore up the floorboards in the house, they found the skeleton of the unfortunate mother: It had been cleared clean of all flesh. The poor woman must have been possessed and devoured by the bakeneko.

The second legend took place in the Hizen Province, in the westernmost corner of Japan, in the household of the daimyō Nabeshima Mitsushige (1632–1700). The daimyō had just executed his retainer, Ryūzōji Matashichirō, because he displeased him during a board game. Ryūzōji's mother, unable to console herself after her son's death, committed suicide, having confided her sorrows in her pet cat. As she was dying, the cat licked the woman's blood and became the bakeneko.

The cat sneaked into Nabeshima Mitsushige's castle. There, he started tormenting the daimyō, so that he couldn't sleep for nights on end. Finally, Mitsushige's new retainer killed the cat, ridding his lord of the trouble.

This story became very popular in Japan, to the point where in the mid-19th century, numerous dramatizations of the story were written, which was then followed by films in the 20th century.

Kitsune

The kitsune are supernatural foxes that grow wiser the older they get—and they can grow quite old, often more than 50 or even 100 years. They can shapeshift into humans and, though some are mischievous, most are friendly to people, and could even become their guardians, friends, or lovers. The special status of foxes in Japanese culture most likely comes from the fact that they repel rats and can guard rice reserves by burrowing themselves in them.

All kitsune are said to serve Inari Ōkami.

One of the oldest tales involving a kitsune comes from the 9th century. It tells a story of a man who got married and had a child with a beautiful woman who had an odd animosity toward dogs. She was, of course, a kitsune; and her child and their descendants, too, soon turned out to possess similar powers. Unfortunately, they often used them to do evil deeds.

This old story marks the beginning of a trend visible in many kitsune stories that came after: In those, the kitsune would often turn into beautiful women. Those women would often stroll alone at dusk and have 'fox-like' faces: High cheekbones, thin eyebrows, narrow eyes, and face. Sometimes, a woman like that would cast a shadow in the shape of a fox.

But foxes could sometimes, instead of turning into women, possess them. They would often enter the bodies of young girls through the tips of their fingers (crawling under their fingernails) or through their breasts. Although sometimes the possession would be a peaceful one, causing the victim only to slightly change their facial expression and, sometimes, even to gain wisdom, most of the occurrences are said to be violent in nature. The victims would show signs of madness, such as frothing at the mouth, running around naked, or speaking and writing in an unknown language (Hearn,

1988). The only way to rid the victim of the fox spirit would be to perform an exorcism at the shrine of Inari Ōkami; if it failed, the victim could even be beaten to death in order to drive the spirit away, and if even that failed, the whole family of the victim could be ostracized by society (Hearn, 1988). Even today, a psychiatric condition known as kitsunetsuki, in which a patient believes to have been possessed by a fox, is being diagnosed in Japan—it is endemic to Japanese culture, which shows how a system of beliefs can affect not only a person's worldview but also their mental health (Haviland, 1999).

Kodama

The kodama are the spirits of the trees, or, perhaps more accurately, shapeshifting trees. They can travel around mountain slopes however much they wish, but their tree always provides a safe haven for them.

Outwardly, the kodama trees look like ordinary trees, but they become cursed when a person attempts to cut them down. Sometimes, blood could even pour out of them if they are hurt by an ax. Usually, a knowledge of which trees in a given area are kodama trees would be passed from generation to generation.

When traveling, the kodama can take on an appearance of eerie lights or animals, but they can also sometimes turn into humans.

Mujina

The mujina are shapeshifting badgers. They are closely related to the tanuki—the raccoon dogs—of whom we'll talk about in a bit. In their natural form, the Mujina are mostly harmless, if a bit mischievous: They would often produce music drumming on their inflated bellies, and create fairy lights.

But the trouble starts when they shapeshift. The belief is that they can turn into almost anything, and there are some forms in which they are definitely more dangerous than others. If they turn into a woman, they can seduce men. One of the earliest accounts mentioning a mujina, the *Nihon Shoki*, mentions that they can turn into women and sing seductive songs (Aston, 2013).

The mujina's favorite form, however, is purportedly that of a Buddhist monk clad in black robes, with an inverted lotus leaf on his head. In this form, they would live underneath a temple, causing mischief.

Sometimes, the mujina can even turn into objects or buildings. In one folk story, a mujina turned into a house in which an unsuspecting traveler stayed during the night and then scared him out of his wits (Harada, 1976). The main reason for those numerous and often fantastical transformations is supposedly that the mujina like to test the extent of their shapeshifting powers and see how perfectly they can imitate objects or people's mannerisms. However, it is said that only a man of real integrity would be capable of telling an ordinary person or an object from a mujina.

Even though they are tricksters, the mujina know the meaning of gratitude. In one story, a man who had been feeding a family of badgers for some time, was later saved by two of them when burglars broke into his house and threatened his life (Casal, 1959). The badgers transformed into giant sumo wrestlers and scared the burglars away.

The mujina are slow to anger, but if they get furious, they are a force to be reckoned with. If their den gets destroyed or their family member killed, the mujina can use their shapeshifting powers to confuse the perpetrator and cause their death, luring them to a fatal accident through a series of transformations.

Tanuki

Tanuki, also known as bake-danuki, are supernatural raccoon dogs. They are closely related to the mujina and share some of their traits, such as turning into women and singing songs or deceiving men. It is believed that before the arrival of Buddhism in Japan, the tanuki were considered divine, but they lost such status after the implementation of new religious beliefs onto the archipelago.

The tanuki are predominantly pranksters. In many folktales—we will learn some of them in the next chapter—they are presented as foolish and comical. Although they have better skills at shapeshifting than, say, the kitsune, they mostly only use those skills for fun. Their comical image is further established by the way they are often depicted: With large scrotums, using their testicles as drums or flung over their backs like traveler's packs.

There are several famous tanuki in Japanese folktales. The most well-known form is a triad of "three famous tanuki of Japan:"

Danzaburou-danuki

The tale of Danzaburou-danuki comes from Sado Island in the eastern part of the Japanese archipelago. It is hard to track the origin of the tale, as it was passed down through generations orally.

Danzaburou-danuki was the chief commander of all the tanuki on Sado Island. He liked playing tricks: Transforming into a wall and blocking people's passage, producing fake golden leaves and then selling them as real ones—and many others.

Despite all this, he wasn't malicious. He was just as likely to lend money to people in need as he was to trick the greedy ones. But he didn't like to share his power; Sado Island doesn't have any foxes on it anymore, and there are several stories relating how Danzaburou-danuki drove away all the kitsune from there.

One day, a kitsune wanted to cross the sea to Sado Island, and so he asked Danzaburou-danuki for a safe passage. The tanuki, having no wish to let the kitsune live on Sado, decided to go for a trick. He told the fox to shapeshift into zōri (thonged Japanese sandals), which he then put on his feet. It was a perfect disguise, he explained: Nobody would suspect a thing.

But, as they were already crossing the sea, Danzaburou-danuki tossed the sandals into the sea, and the kitsune, who didn't manage to shapeshift back to his real form in time, drowned. From that point on, no kitsune tried to settle on Sato.

Shibaemon-tanuki

The legend of Shibaemon-tanuki comes from Awaji Island. In behavior, Shibaemon-tanuki was very similar to Danzaburou-danuki. He liked drumming his belly and selling fake golden leaves, disguised as a human. To balance out the chaos, he would also guide lost travelers through the pathways around Mount Mikuma, where he lived with his wife.

One day, Shibaemon-tanuki decided to go to Osaka and watch a famous play. So, he disguised himself as a man, and his wife as a woman, and they set off on their journey.

They were like a pair of overexcited tourists: They had never been to Osaka before, and they were dazzled by the bustling city. In the middle of sightseeing, they decided to hold a contest of disguises.

First, Shibaemon's wife turned herself into an attendant in a procession led by a daimyō. Shibaemon's task was to recognize her in the crowd, which he did, although it was difficult since her disguise was near-perfect.

When it came to Shibaemon's turn, he spotted a procession of feudal lords. When his wife saw the procession, she approached one of the lords immediately. "Oh, you're good," she said, "but I recognized you."

This proved to be a mistake: The man was not, in fact, Shibaemon, but a real lord. For her impudence, the poor woman was struck down and killed where she stood.

Shibaemon was struck with grief. However, he still had a play to see, and he decided he didn't want to waste his ticket. So, he went into the theater; but unfortunately, somebody in the audience had brought a massive dog. Shibaemon was immediately scared of it but managed to suppress his fear.

That is until the dog started barking at him. Startled, Shibaemon turned uncontrollably into his tanuki form, in which the dog killed him. News traveled far and wide from Osaka of a tanuki killed by a dog; and when the inhabitants of a small village by the slopes of Mount Mikuma heard this, and then they didn't hear Shibaemon drumming his belly anymore, they immediately knew that he was dead.

Yashima no Hage-tanuki

Yashima came from a town of the same name, which is now a district of Takamatsu City in Japan. The story of his life is tied to that of the patriarch of the Taira clan, Taira no Shigemori (1138–1179), who was said to have saved the tanuki's ancestor from an arrow wound. As a show of gratitude, the tanuki and his descendants protected the Taira clan, and when it went into oblivion, they became the protectors of one of the temples which the clan had founded.

And that is when Yashima no Hage-tanuki's life started. He was the protector of the temple and, thanks to his mastery of disguises, he became the chief of all tanuki in the area. He would create mirages in the air and show them to people, and, of course, his power of shapeshifting was without contest.

One day, Yashima was challenged by no other than Shibaemon-tanuki. He boasted that he was the best shapeshifter in Japan, and so, the two tanuki met and decided to challenge themselves to a contest of disguises.

On the morning of the contest, Shibaemon awoke and, to his horror, saw a massive fleet sailing on the sea on the horizon. He cried out in alarm, thinking that a war was coming; but as soon as he did, the fleet disappeared and Yashima appeared before him: The fleet had been his disguise. Yashima, glad that he had won, started boasting about his victory far and wide.

But Shibaemon was far from being done. Remembering the misfortune with his wife (and, in this version of the tale, not being dead yet), he now did the same thing to

Yashima. He seemingly disguised himself as a member of an entourage of a daimyō, and when Yashima cried out and approached one of the soldiers, he was instantly struck with a spear for his insolence. The soldier, of course, had been a real one.

Shibaemon, as an act of courtesy, threw Yashima a funeral. After his death, Yashima's spirit started possessing people. However, he wasn't malicious; instead, he mediated between people and helped them out.

Tsukumogami

The tsukumogami are a special kind of shapeshifters: Everyday objects, especially tools, that acquired supernatural abilities. A popular belief is that any object which is older than 100 years would acquire self-awareness and become alive—although that number by itself might not always be literal but a symbol of a thing being very old.

What happens when an object becomes a tsukumogami? Like other types of shapeshifters, it could turn into a human of any age or gender; into a spirit; or into an animal. It seems that those shapeshifters would later become mostly deceiving and mischievous in nature so people would mostly try to get rid of old things.

As Buddhism came to Japan, the traditional Shinto belief in the Tsukumogami became merged with the Buddhist belief in reincarnation, and so the sentient objects started to be seen as reincarnated souls of those who did not manage to attain enlightenment. Today, this symbolic meaning of the tsukumogami is mostly lost, and they permeated Japanese popular culture, appearing in anime, manga, books, and films.

There are different types of tsukumogami. Some examples include: Abumi-guchi (a furry monster emerging from a stirrup of a dead soldier); Bakezōri (a possessed sandal that makes noise around the house); Biwa-bokuboku (a sentient biwa, that is a Japanese lute); Boroboroton (an animated futon which attempts to strangle its owner at night); Chōchin-obake (a possessed lantern); and Ungaikyō (possessed mirror which shows a monstrous reflection of those who look into it).

The Yōkai

The yōkai is perhaps the broadest category of supernatural beings in Japanese folklore. In some ways, the obake could also be classified as a type of yōkai. Most broadly speaking, the yōkai are spirits: All supernatural creatures that aren't gods. They aren't demons; instead, they can be both benevolent or malevolent, or simply mischievous.

There is an almost innumerable amount of various yōkai in different regional tales from Japan. Below is the selection of those most famous, interesting, or sometimes even astonishing.

Abura-akago

Abura-akago is a child-like spirit. It lives inside andon lamps—traditional Japanese cubical hanging lamps which could be found both at homes and in temples. When in a lamp, this spirit licks and eats the oil inside; but it can also travel between lamps in the form of a ball of fire. In that latter form, they can haunt the crossroads, confusing the travelers who walk in the dark.

Aka Manto

Aka Manto is perhaps the most peculiar yōkai. The belief in it is widespread in modern Japan and it is more often described as an urban legend than a folklore figure; however, urban legends are mostly just folklore transposed into modern times.

So, who is Aka Manto? It is a spirit living in public bathrooms. It wears a red cloak and a mask and is always equipped with a blue and a red roll of toilet paper. It appears in bathrooms whenever someone occupies a stall; some say that it most often happens in female bathrooms, as the spirit is male; and mostly to those who chose the last stall in a row.

Aka Manto would then ask the victim a question: Would they prefer a blue or a red roll of paper? This has to be ignored, as either choice would mean the victim's death: The red roll means laceration and getting drowned in one's own blood, and the blue one means strangulation and all the blood being sucked out of one's body. So, unsurprisingly, getting out of the bathroom stall as soon as possible and running away is the best option.

It is said that some people tried to outsmart the Aka Manto. They would say that they preferred a roll in a different color. But that doesn't end well either; the spirit could then drag the victim's body to the spirit world. Specifically, if a victim said they preferred yellow paper, their head could be forced into the toilet and they could drown.

The belief in Aka Manto most likely started in the 1930s, specifically among children and teenagers in public schools (Meyer, 2016). It isn't difficult to imagine a school prankster standing behind the belief. But however it started, the odd but dangerous spirit of the public bathrooms now entered the world of the Japanese supernatural.

Akaname

Continuing with the scatological theme—Akaname is a filthy, green monster the size of a child's stature that licks filth from bathtubs and bathrooms. It is literally born out of filth in bathrooms that have been neglected.

Although Akaname is ugly and unpleasant to see, it doesn't harm people; it contents itself with licking filth. The unpleasantness of the creature, however, is enough to spur people into keeping their bathrooms clean.

Akugyo

Akugyo is an aquatic yōkai—a sea monster if you will. It's a giant fish that mostly lives in the southern seas by the shores of the Japanese archipelago. It doesn't seem to be actively malicious towards people; however, its size means that boats can often get stuck between their fins and destroyed.

Amabie

Amabie, broadly speaking, is the Japanese equivalent of a mermaid or a merman. It is slightly different in appearance from the merpeople from European traditions: It has three fin-like legs and a beak-like mouth. It also has the power of prophecy, it can emerge from the sea and predict either a good harvest or an epidemic. Amabie's presence was reported at various points in Japanese history, usually before natural disasters occurred.

There are also different variants of the Amabie. Some can cry out like apes, others glow in the dark; yet others can put on a monk's garb and would pass as monks, if not for their three legs.

Recently, Amabie had a bit of a resurgence because of the COVID-19 pandemic. The image of the creature warning against the disease became quite popular in Japanese social media (Alt, 2020).

Hone-onna

Hone-onna's name literally means "bone woman." Her existence is attested in one folk story in which an animated female skeleton visited a man whom she used to be in love with when alive. She would visit him every night and stay away until the morning; the man didn't realize that the creature was a skeleton, and not a woman herself, since she had put on a disguise. He only realized what was going on when a neighbor peeked into his bedroom and spotted him embracing a skeleton.

Kappa

Kappa, one of the best-known yōkai in Japan, is a reptile-like creature with humanoid features which lives in rivers and ponds. It is the size of a small child, and yet, it possesses considerable strength as it likes engaging in sumo wrestling. Its skin is scaly and slimy save for its back, where it wears a turtle shell. Its hands and legs are webbed, and on the top of its head, it has a small indent, in which the water in which it lives is accumulated.

Although Kappa is a yōkai, it demands people to worship it like a god and can get considerably angry when they don't comply. It would typically attack its victims in water, and remove their organs through their anus. It can also devour whole men and rape women who come to bathe in rivers. More mundanely, a Kappa would also cause drowning—for which reason it has often been used as a cautionary tale for children to prevent them from swimming in deep and treacherous waters (Ashkenazi, 2008).

In order to placate a Kappa, an offering of a cucumber—its favorite food—should be made. In more dire and desperate circumstances, there are a few ways to survive an encounter with a Kappa. Firstly, since it likes when people are polite, one should bow to it, and it would return the bow; then, the water which is accumulated in the indent on the top of its head would spill, and it wouldn't be able to straighten until the water is refilled. During this time, the victim might make their escape—or they can refill the indent, after which the Kappa would be forced to serve the person until the end of their days.

A different method is slightly more dangerous: To engage in sumo wrestling with the Kappa and use this opportunity to spill the water from its indent.

Once a Kappa is forced to serve a human, it would irrigate their fields and bring them fresh fish; they could also cure various diseases, as their affinity for removing organs from their victims also means they are quite skilled in medicine.

Nure-onna

Nure-onna is a hybrid: A creature with the body of a snake and the head of a woman. Nure-onna's hair is always wet, and it lives in rivers and seas, where it often lures sailors to their death. There are different ways in which it can do that. It can appear to be a young woman washing her hair in the water or drowning, which then turns out to be a deadly snake when the sailors come closer; or, alternatively, it can hand over a sleeping baby to a man, begging him to hold it for her—but when the baby is already in the man's arms, it turns into a heavy stone which he can't drop, and he drowns, or a Nure-onna eats him. There is only one way to prevent oneself from that fate, and that is, to wear slippery gloves.

Shuten Dōji

Shuten Dōji is a special case on our list: Rather than being a category of being, he was an individual, a powerful leader of spirits or demons (*oni* in Japanese, which is a special, usually malicious, subcategory of yōkai), who got defeated by Minamoto no Yorimitsu, the same leader who employed Kintarō. The story about their showdown was described in a 14th-century text and goes as follows (Reider, 2010):

Shuten Dōji lived near Kyoto, during the times of Emperor Ichijō (986–1011). He would lure and kidnap young maidens. When this fact was noticed in Kyoto, an investigation started, until at last the emperor's advisors established that it was Shuten Dōji, the king of the spirits, who was responsible. So, the emperor commanded

Minamoto no Yorimitsu to take a crew and go on an expedition to get rid of the monster.

Minamoto left Kyoto in 995. On his way, he and his party met various gods disguised as human helpers; they advised them to disguise themselves as yamabushi—ascetic monks. Thus, they could approach Mount Ōe where Shuten Dōji lived unobserved.

As they approached, the party met an old washerwoman who was doing laundry by the river. They asked her for the whereabouts of the demons, and she said that they were near. She also explained that she had been kidnapped by Dōji when she was young, and forced into servitude. Most girls were met with the same fate; however, some of them had been ripped apart and devoured by Dōji's pack of demons.

The party moved forward until they finally found Dōji's lair. Pretending to be priests, they asked for lodgings. The demon, even though he was wicked, couldn't really refuse the holy men. He invited them inside and gave them a drink of sake, then told them his version of the story: How he and his band of demons had been driven away from nearby Hira Mountains, and how they did everything they could to survive. It was quite a sorry tale, but it didn't negate the fact that the demons had been kidnapping young women.

Then, Minamoto shared his own sake with Dōji. It was a drink given to him by one of the disguised gods—much stronger than regular sake. As Dōji and his demons fell asleep, Minamoto and his party dressed back in their armor and attacked the defenseless hosts. The disguised gods came to their aid and held down Dōji as Minamoto hacked his head off.

But this wasn't the end of Dōji; his head was still alive and biting after being cut off. It jumped at Minamoto's head, but thankfully, he had been wearing a double helmet, so the demon's sharp teeth didn't manage to cut through it. Soon, the head stopped biting and the demons were defeated. The warriors then set free the maidens who were being held hostage.

Tengu

The Tengu is a spirit rather hard to define. He can take on many forms, from a large bird to a monkey, but he usually has a humanoid face with a long nose or a beak. What he likes most, however, is putting on the garb of a priest, especially of the ascetic yamabushi, and impersonating him. In this form, Tengu was most likely borrowed from Chinese folklore (de Visser, 1908).

What is Tengu's specialty? As a monk impersonator, he most often has malicious intent; he is the enemy of

Buddhism, and often robs temples, leads priests astray, or kidnaps them (although they usually don't vanish without a trace, just end up miles away from the places they've been in before). Sometimes, he would even possess women and, in that form, try to seduce holy men. The belief is that Tengu himself is a spirit of a monk who was unholy during his life.

One interesting story featuring a Tengu was written down in the 12th century, in the war chronicle *Hōgen Monogatari* (de Visser, 1908). It tells the story of Emperor Sutoku (1119–1164), who was supposed to become a Tengu after his death. After being deposed from the throne and having raised a rebellion, he died in torment and swore to come back as an angry demon.

However, not all Tengu are bad. Over time, the image of the spirit shifted from that of a destroyer of temples to their protector. In the 18th and 19th centuries, the Tengu appeared in many folktales as protectors of forests (de Visser, 1908).

They also changed their appearance from fearsome to slightly comedic spirits. For example, in one folktale a Tengu lost one of his attributes—a fan that could enlarge people's noises—to a little mischievous boy (Seki, 1966). The boy then used the fan to extend the nose of a nobleman's daughter and promised to change it back to a normal shape in exchange for her hand in marriage. But his pranks finally caught up with him: As he was falling asleep one day, he accidentally used the fan on himself and his nose got so long that it reached the heavens.

Yamauba

Yamauba is a female spirit. She lives in forests and would take on the appearance of a young beautiful woman washing or combing her long black hair. Sometimes, if a hunter accidentally shoots in her direction, she would catch his bullet in her hands. But the youthful appearance is only a deception: In reality, Yamauba is an old crone and a dangerous one at that. She delights in eating little children. However, some of the children are special and Yamauba would rather raise them—the mountain witch who raised Kintarō is said to have been a Yamauba.

In general, there are two conflicting portrayals of a Yamauba: As a dangerous witch-eating traveler, and as a supernatural helper who would help out those who are unfortunate. Embodying this second portrayal is a short tale of two stepsisters who were gathering fruit in a forest. The older sister was kind, even though she suffered torment from her stepmother; the younger sister was cruel and selfish. A Yamauba then appeared and gave the older sister a sack full of treasure, while cursing the younger sister to an unhappy fate.

The Yūrei

The yūrei can also be classified as a type of yōkai—however, a very specific type. They are the closest to what we would call ghosts, the spirits of dead people. Even though the Shinto religion doesn't hold very specific views on the afterlife—except that a spirit of a good person would eventually join their ancestors—there is a belief that ghosts of those who died a violent death (such as murder or suicide) would then haunt the living, sometimes to enact revenge for their sudden death. There are some common characteristics of a yūrei: White clothing and long, black, disheveled hair; the lack of feet (they instead float in the air), and lifelessly dangling hands.

Funayūrei

The Funayūrei are vengeful spirits of those who died at sea. Since they drowned in shipwrecks, they want the living sailors to join them, so they would often use ladles to fill boats with water and sink them. Some of them would even form crews and sail through the sea in ghost ships. They usually use bad weather—rains, storms, fog—to lure sailors to their deaths. Sometimes, they tamper with the ship's compasses.

There are several ways to defeat the Funayūrei. Some accounts state that one has to stop one's ship immediately and stare at the ghost; others, that one has to stir the water and startle it. Some objects thrown into the sea are also said to distract and repel the Funayūrei: Flowers, incense sticks, or rice.

Depending on the region, there are different types of Funayūrei that have been spotted over the centuries. For example, around the region of Kyushu, a Funayūrei called Ugume would pretend to be a ship or an island, and it would steer sailors off their course. It could be repelled by throwing ash into the water or by smoking tobacco.

Goryō

The Goryō are the vengeful spirits of aristocrats. Most of them are said to have died as a result of a famine, disease, or murder… And they are also believed to be capable of bringing about the misfortunes that ended their life. For this reason, the Goryō are often worshiped in shrines as a preemptive measure. Some can even become gods—as was the case with Tenjin, whom we've already met.

Ikiryō

The Ikiryō are a bit of a special case: They are disembodied spirits who left people who are still alive. It is a belief that a person who experiences very violent emotions, especially holding a grudge against someone, can unleash an Ikiryō who can later haunt their victim, even over a large distance. They also have the power to curse or possess the other person.

But sometimes, not only vengeance brings about the Ikiryō. Extreme feelings of love, infatuation, and obsession can also be the cause. In one tale, a teenage boy by the name of Matsunosuke was possessed by the spirits of two women who were in love with him, and he would talk to them even though they were not there physically; they would also cause him to fly up in the air. Only an exorcism from a priest delivered the boy from his condition.

During the Edo Period, the separation of the soul from the body by creating an Ikiryō was considered an illness (Hearn, 2020). It was believed that an out-of-body experience was a part of that condition, as well as seeing one's identical double.

Kuchisake-onna

Kuchisake-onna is a singular spirit. It is said that during her life, she was a beautiful woman who got disfigured horribly.

Her husband was a samurai, and spent most of his time away from home; Kuchisake grew lonely and started an affair. When her husband learned about this, he enacted a truly cruel punishment: He cut her mouth from ear to ear.

It is no wonder that after her death, Kuchisake became a vengeful spirit. She would roam the streets with her face covered by a mask, with a knife in her hand. She would accost her victims and ask them, "Am I beautiful?" If a person responds negatively, she would kill them; if affirmative, she would take off her mask and show her mutilated face, asking, "Even now?" If the victim screams in fear or says "No, now you are not beautiful," she would cut them with her knife in half. If, however, they say "Yes," Kuchisake-onna would take out a pair of scissors and cut the victim's mouth so that it resembles hers.

There are a few ways to survive an encounter with Kuchisake-onna unscathed. One can distract her by throwing money or candies at her; or one can cleverly respond to her questions, saying that she is neither beautiful nor ugly, but average; when Kuchisake ponders on that answer, her victim might be able to run away.

Oiwa

The story of Oiwa might be the most popular Japanese ghost story ever created. It is a story about betrayal that carries even beyond the grave, which is said to have historical basis in the 17th century (*Oiwa*, n.d.).

Oiwa was a young girl married to a samurai by the name of Iemon, who was unhappy in that marriage. Iemon did not act according to the samurai code and was instead a thief and a wasteful man. So one day, Oiwa said to herself that enough was enough, and she decided to separate with him and return to her family home.

But Iemon was not also a man without honor, but also quick to anger. He ran after Oiwa, presumably intent on dragging her back to his home by force. However, on the road, he was stopped by Oiwa's father, Yotsuya Samon. Samon knew all about Iemon's misconduct with his daughter and demanded that Samon divorce Oiwa and let her come back to her family.

Iemon wouldn't have this. He murdered Samon where he stood and then pursued Oiwa. He now put on a weeping act: He reported that Samon had been murdered on the road by a ruffian; then, he swore revenge on that imagined man and begged Oiwa to reconcile with him and help him find the murderer. Oiwa, stricken by grief, agreed.

They lived together for some time until Oiwa became pregnant. It was a hard time since, due to Iemon's poor management, they were destitute. Oiwa's pregnancy was difficult, and there was hardly any money for doctors; she managed to give birth to a healthy child but became sickly herself. As might be suspected of a bad husband, Iemon wasn't at all concerned for Oiwa; instead, he came to resent her, because she lost her beauty.

But soon, another factor came into play: Next to Iemon and Oiwa's house lived a rich doctor who had a beautiful daughter, Oume. Oume fell in love with Iemon and dearly wished to marry him, which she confided in her father. The doctor was clever and decided to help his daughter in a most immoral way.

He pretended to prescribe a special ointment for Oiwa— but in reality, it was poison that was supposed to leave her with a disfigured face. Poor Oiwa had no idea what she was taking—and even after applying the ointment, she didn't look in the mirror, so she had no idea what happened.

As suspected, Iemon now not only was distant towards his wife; he actively hated her. At the same time, the doctor came to him and persuaded him to divorce Oiwa and marry his daughter instead; he also promised him all his family fortune if he did so. Iemon agreed; and soon, he started selling all his family possessions, including Oiwa's and their child's clothes, to be able to afford the pompous marriage to Oume.

But Iemon decided to behave even more cruelly. He still didn't have a legal reason to divorce Oiwa: Her lack of beauty was definitely not enough. So, he hired a friend, Takuetsu, who agreed to rape her, and wanted to later accuse her of infidelity.

The next night, Takuetsu broke into Oiwa's bedroom. As he approached her, she screamed and accidentally uncovered her face; upon seeing it, Takuetsu was terrified and immediately abandoned his plan. He talked to Oiwa and explained everything; after which, he showed her her own reflection in a mirror.

Oiwa's horror was hard to behold. Frantically, she tried to cover the scarred part of her face with her hair, but as she started brushing it, it fell out in clumps. Then, she started screaming; in a flash, she understood all the ways in which she had been wronged by Iemon. In a bout of madness, she reached into a cupboard and pulled out a sword. Then, she thrust it into her own throat.

Oiwa fell to the floor; Takuetsu, terrified, fled the scene. As Oiwa was bleeding to death, she cursed Iemon's name till her last breath.

But when a serving girl discovered Oiwa's body and related the news to Iemon, the cruel samurai couldn't quite conceal his contentment. The servant soon became suspicious, so quickly, Iemon killed her, and disposed of her body along with Oiwa's. In his maliciousness and stupidity, he was thinking that now, he was finally free to marry Oume and that all his troubles were behind him.

But Oiwa's curse was already in place. On his wedding night, Iemon couldn't sleep; as he tossed and turned in his bed, he suddenly saw Oiwa's disfigured face. Terrified, he reached for his sword and slashed at the apparition, only for it to disappear and reveal that he had in reality killed his new wife, Oume.

He didn't know what to do. He jumped from his bed and decided to get help from his new father-in-law; maybe the doctor could still help Oume. But as he ran, he suddenly saw the ghost of the murdered serving girl before him; again, he slashed at it with his sword, only to discover that he had killed his father-in-law.

Iemon ran and ran, but everywhere, Oiwa's ghost pursued him. It hid behind every corner, looked at him from paper lanterns, and stood in his way when he walked down the streets. In the end, he escaped to a hermitage high up in the mountains—but even there, Oiwa's ghost haunted him. He could no longer tell what was real and what was not; in the end, he went mad, and soon after, died.

The tragic story of Oiwa remained in oral tradition until 1825, when it was dramatized by Tsuruya Nanboku (1755–1829) in a form of a kabuki play (a traditional Japanese dance-drama), under the name *Tōkaidō Yotsuya Kaidan* (*Ghost story of Yotsuya in Tokaido*) (*Yotsuya Kaidan*, n.d.). It had multiple film adaptations in the 20th century.

Okiku

Okiku is another girl whose tragic fate became a popular and dramatized ghost story. It was initially a folk story which was later adapted into a bunraku (puppet) play in 1741 (Monnet, 1993).

Okiku was a serving girl. As, sadly, is often the case in situations like these, her master, a samurai by the name of Aoyama Tessan, got infatuated with her and was making rather forceful advances on her, claiming that he wanted to marry her. However, Okiku refused.

Scorned, Aoyama decided to take his revenge. He hid one of the very precious Delft plates (earthenware imported from the Netherlands) and made Okiku believe that she had lost it. A crime for losing such a precious possession would be death.

Okiku frantically counted and recounted the plates, but the one missing was nowhere to be found. She had no other choice than to confess her perceived crime, so she went to Aoyama and told him everything.

Now, the samurai decided to enact his plan. He pretended to be magnanimous and offered to overlook the whole matter if Okiku decided to become his lover.

But Okiku still refused. Enraged, Aoyama pushed her down a well, where she fell to her death.

But this was by no means the end of the story. Okiku came back as a ghost and tormented Aoyama. She would count to nine—recounting the Delft plates—and then emit a great shriek instead of the number ten, which represented the tenth plate she had supposedly lost. Aoyama couldn't get rid of the ghost until he found a priest who exorcized the ghost through a special ritual and by shouting "Ten!" loudly at the apparition.

Over the years, the story acquired many adaptations. Some of them had Aoyama peacefully contemplating his mistake; others, him committing suicide out of madness. A belief was formed that Okiku's ghost hadn't been exorcized, but instead haunted the wells.

Ubume

With the Ubume, we are coming back to categories of spirits rather than individual apparitions. They are ghosts of women who died pregnant or during childbirth. They would roam the streets, carrying bundles in their hands which, at first glance, resemble a swaddled child. However, when an Ubume would try to give away the bundle to a passer-by, they would quickly discover that it is only a rock wrapped in cloth. The rock would become heavier and heavier until it's impossible to hold, causing damage.

There was a way of preventing a woman from becoming an Ubume. If she died during childbirth and the child died as well, one had to bury her with the child in her arms—or, if the child was still in her womb, one had to cut it out and put it into her arms. If this was impossible, putting a doll in a woman's arms was an option.

Zashiki-warashi

The folk stories about Zashiki-warashi come mostly from the Iwate Prefecture. Those spirits are said to live in storage rooms, and they are mostly harmless, if not auspicious. They are said to bring good fortune to the families in whose houses they live.

Zashiki-warashi can be both male and female. They have red faces and short-cropped hair, and they live from three to fifteen years. They would often perform mild pranks in the household they live in, such as making rustling sounds or leaving footprints in ash or bleach powder.

Other Supernatural Creatures

There are some creatures in Japanese folklore that aren't easily classifiable: Hybrids; not-quite-gods but not spirits either… Let us now learn their stories.

Kirin

Kirin was originally a Chinese creature, known as Qilin; from there, it traveled to Japan, Korea, and Vietnam. It's a hybrid: It has horse-like hooves and the body of a Chinese dragon, as well as antlers on its head. However, in Japan, it is depicted as more deer-like than dragon-like.

In China, Kirin is considered a portent of someone very wise being born, be it a sage or a ruler. It retained its position as a good sign in Japan.

Komainu

The Komainu are another type of hybrid creatures: Half-lions, half-dogs. Their statues guard Shinto temples. There are two types of Komainu: Those that guard the entrances and those that are kept inside, in spaces not available to the public. They are supposed to repel the evil spirits from holy places.

Kyonshii

Kyonshii is yet another creature borrowed from Chinese culture—it is a special type of vampire known in China as Jiangshi. It's an animated corpse: Very stiff and dressed in a shroud, it moves around by hopping with its arms outstretched. It doesn't drink blood, however; instead, it sucks out people's life force.

There are many ways one can use to repel the kyonshii. Some of them include: Swatting it with a broom; holding one's breath; or dropping a bag of coins and thus distracting it, so it starts counting the coins instead of pursuing its victim.

Mizuchi

Mizuchi is a Japanese dragon. It is strongly connected to the aquatic dragon deities, such as Okami. Over time, it became conflated with creatures such as the Kappa.

Mizuchi is first mentioned in the chronicle *Nihon Shoki* as dwelling in the Takahashi River and poisoning the water (Aston, 2013).

Over time, several cases of seeing a Mizuchi have been reported, and most possibly, not all of them were referencing a singular creature, but rather, a category of creatures. In another story from the *Nihon Shoki*, a man named Agatamori was supposed to have defeated a Mizuchi (Aston, 2013). He came near a pool and threw three white-flowered gourds (or long melons—very light and bottle-shaped fruits) into the water, challenging the Mizuchi to drown them. Because the fruits were so light, the dragon couldn't sink them with his mighty claws; so he resorted to transformation and changed himself into a deer. That was the moment Agatamori was waiting for: He shot the deer with his arrow, killing it.

Namazu

Namazu is a peculiar monster: It is a giant catfish that lives deep in the water in the center of the earth. Its movements often cause earthquakes. It belongs to the god of thunder Takemikazuchi, who frequently tries to tame it; but when he lets his guard down, the fish thrashes and causes trouble.

It is believed that the connection between a giant fish and an earthquake came from an observation of catfish getting unusually active and restless before earthquakes, a fact that was later scientifically proven (*Sensitivity*, 1933).

Chapter 7:

Folktales

Throughout this book, I have told you many myths and folktales connected to gods, heroes, and supernatural creatures. But in this last chapter, we will learn stories that we haven't heard before—and which form the corpus of some of the most celebrated tales from Japanese traditional imagination. Many of them will be stories of ordinary people meeting unusual ends—and either emerging successful, or losing everything. They were written down in a traditional Japanese art form known as the monogatari—a prose narrative similar to a novel.

The Tale of the Bamboo Cutter

Our first tale is one of the earliest known written monogatari—it was composed either in the 9th or 10th century (Keene, 1993). It tells a tale of how an ordinary man found a supernatural princess.

There once was a bamboo cutter by the name of Taketori no Okina. He was an old man who toiled away day by day, earning his meager income. But one day was special for him; as he was cutting the bamboo, he came across an unusual shiny stick. When he cut it, he saw a little girl sleeping inside; she was no bigger than the size of a thumb.

The cutter and his wife didn't have their own children, so, as is often the case in these types of stories, they decided to take the girl home and raise her as their own child. They named her Nayotake no Kaguya-hime (which literally meant "Shining Princess of the Young Bamboo").

From that point on, every time Taketori cut a new bamboo stalk in the forest, he would find a gold piece in it. This improved his family situation considerably; soon, he was rich.

Nayotake also grew very quickly. In only three months, she transformed from a child into a beautiful young woman. Soon, news traveled far and wide about a beautiful maiden and an heiress to a fortune; although Taketori and his wife initially tried to shelter Nayotake from suitors, it soon proved futile.

Among others, five nobles arrived at Taketori's house, all intent on marrying Nayotake: Prince Ishitskuri, Prince

Kuramochi, Minister Abe no Mimuraji, Grand Counselor Ōtomo no Miyuki, and the Middle Counselor Isonokami no Marotari. Taketori, after some persuading, agreed for Nayotake to choose between them.

But Nayotake wasn't interested in any of them. Not wanting to offend them by rejecting them outright, she devised five tasks which were, nonetheless, impossible to complete. They were all about bringing five objects which no mortal should touch or even see: The begging bowl of the Buddha; a branch made of jewels that only grew on a mythical island of Hōrai; a robe made of skins of Chinese mythical fire rats; a jewel from a dragon's neck; and finally, an impossible object: A cowry shell born of a swallow.

Initially, all the nobles dispersed in pursuit of their tasks. But very soon, they realized how impossible the tasks were, and decided to cheat. Prince Ishitskuri gave Nayotake a fake stone bowl; Prince Kuramochi gave her a branch laid out with Japan's finest jewels, which nonetheless were by no means mythical; the Minister bought a robe from a Chinese merchant, but didn't test it for being fireproof; the Grand Counselor honestly tried to pursue a dragon, but was deterred by a storm; and the Middle Counselor fell down a cliff when trying to reach to a swallow's nest, and died.

When three out of five suitors came back to Nayotake, she saw through their deceit immediately. The bowl didn't reflect the holy light of the Buddha; finding a merchant who had sold Kuramochi the jewels wasn't a difficult task; and the Minister's robe burned immediately in the fire. Disgusted, Nayotake sent the suitors away.

And then, an extraordinary thing happened: The Emperor of Japan himself came to Nayotake's house and proposed. When she saw him, she was immediately taken to him and didn't burden him with an impossible task. However, she still told him she couldn't marry him, because she wasn't a native of his country; she had come from a different place.

The Emperor drove away, but he kept in contact with Nayotake through letters for three long years. In the meantime, the girl grew more and more restless; every full moon, she would cry, and wouldn't respond to the bamboo cutter's questions. At last, when she became more and more upset, she revealed the truth: She had come from the Moon, where she was a princess. She had to return to her people, even if they didn't want her; she said that she had committed a crime (whose nature she nonetheless didn't want to reveal), and that is why she had been sent to the Earth as banishment.

Now, Nayotake started preparing for her journey back; she knew that soon, messengers from the Moon would come and get her. Meanwhile, the Emperor sent his escort to protect her from the wrath of the Moon people.

But the protection was clearly not enough; when an embassy from the Moon finally came to get Nayotake, everyone was blinded by an unearthly light and fell to the ground. Nayotake left her robe behind, wanting her foster parents to have something to remember her by; she then put a drop of the Moon elixir of immortality and attached it to a letter to the Emperor. With great pomp, she ascended into the sky.

The bamboo cutter and his wife wept dearly for their daughter whom they grew to love. They became so sad that they got ill. Meanwhile, a messenger came with Nayotake's last letter to the Emperor, relating the news. The Emperor went sick with sadness, and immediately asked his messenger which mountain was the tallest one in Japan, and therefore the closest to the sky.

The messenger told him that the highest peak of the Suruga Province in the south was reportedly the tallest mountain. He had probably expected the Emperor to climb it in order to be closer to his lost love; but instead, the wise monarch ordered the letter and the elixir of immortality to be brought to the mountain peak and burned. He wanted to make his will known to the Moon princess: He was trying to forget about her, and he was rejecting immortality, for it made no sense to never die, and yet be unable to see his love ever again.

And thus ended the melancholy tale of the bamboo cutter and his adopted daughter, the Moon princess.

Bunbuku Chagama

Bunbuku Chagama is a humorous and heartwarming tale about a tanuki and its exploits. The oral fairy tale version of the story was written down in the 19th century (Mitford, 1871).

There was once a chief priest in a temple. Every day in the evening, he liked to drink some tea, and he owned a magnificent tea kettle. But one day, the moment he put the kettle on the hearth, it suddenly started moving, and then sprung out a raccoon-like tail, transforming into a tanuki.

The monk didn't like this turn of events. He employed his novices to subdue the tanuki and kept it in confinement; then, he sold it at a market—thus, having no idea what he lost.

When a peddler bought a seemingly completely ordinary kettle, it transformed into a Tanuki in his hands. The peddler, startled, almost dropped it; but the tanuki said that it would perform acrobatic tricks if the peddler promised to treat it well. The bargain struck, and the peddler went around, showing the tanuki on the roadsides and during circus-like shows. He shared all his food with the creature, and as an exchange, it walked on ropes and spun around to the delight of the spectators.

Soon, the peddler amassed a great fortune—thus proving that whoever meets a tanuki, should do well if they treat it with dignity.

The Crab and the Monkey

The Crab and the Monkey is a story of violence and retribution. It can be read a bit like a parable, or a metaphorical animal fable. It was first published in the 19th century, ending a time of oral transmission (Ozaki, n.d.).

A female crab was once out on a walk. While strolling, she found a rice ball, a true treasure. She presented her findings to her friend, a monkey. But the clever and manipulative creature persuaded her to trade the rice ball for a persimmon seed. The crab wasn't happy about the exchange, but she couldn't find it in herself to refuse.

However, her discontent soon turned to joy when the seed planted in the ground slowly grew into a tree. The crab was now in possession of a fortune that didn't run out immediately.

There was one problem, however: The crab couldn't climb the tree. She had to ask the monkey to do it for her—something that her sly acquaintance decided to exploit. He quickly climbed up, but instead of throwing some of the fruits down for the crab, he started eating all the ripe persimmons. When the crab realized what was happening and started protesting, the monkey threw unripe, hard fruits at her, injuring her. Shocked, the crab, who had been pregnant, gave birth before her time—and then shortly died.

But when the crab's offspring grew up, they decided to take revenge on the greedy and malicious monkey. They amassed unusual allies for their confrontation: A chestnut, a cow dung, a bee, and a heavy mortar. They decided to storm the monkey's house, where they hid, the chestnut in the hearth, the bee in the water container, the cow dung on the floor in an invisible spot, and the mortar on the roof.

The monkey entered his home. Immediately, he went to the hearth and tried to warm himself; but from there, the chestnut jumped, causing him to burn his face. Outraged and in pain, the monkey ran to the container full of water to cool off the burn; but there, the bee was waiting for him and stung him immediately. The monkey was now mad with pain; he ran out of his house, clutching at his burning face; but he didn't see the cow dung on the floor and slipped on it. Then, it was left to the mortar to finish the job. It fell from the roof, crushing the monkey's skull and killing him.

The point of the story is relatively simple: Harsh, retributive justice will come sooner or later for evildoers. The flourish is, however, the unusual use of the animal characters and objects who took part in how justice was served.

The Crane Wife

The Crane Wife, or, *Tsuru Nyōbō*, is a very unusual, and yet heartbreaking, love story. For ages, it circulated in oral tradition and has now many variants, being one of the best-known Japanese folktales (Adams & Seki, 1976).

The story starts simply enough: A man married a beautiful woman, whom he loved dearly. But he had no idea that the woman was a shapeshifting crane. She loved him and decided to make the sacrifice of changing into a human in order to be with him.

The man was a silk merchant. Every night, his wife would weave silk brocade for him, which he would later sell. In order for the brocade to be of extraordinary quality, she used her own crane feathers which she plucked every night. But this made her increasingly weaker.

Soon, she became very sick. Her husband, of course, noticed this and demanded to know what the matter was. Very reluctantly, she told him. She was afraid that his love for her would disappear when he discovered her true nature.

In tears, he said that his love for her didn't diminish. But she had to stop what she'd been doing; he didn't need that kind of sacrifice from her.

But she had been doing this all for them and their love, she responded. For her as a crane, life didn't exist without sacrifices.

The man disagreed. He said that love should be pleasurable, and one didn't have to sacrifice one's own core for it.

The wife frowned. This disagreed with everything she believed in. But instead of arguing further, or trying to understand her husband's point, she turned back into a crane and then flew away. Her husband didn't deserve to be with her if he didn't believe that love requires sacrifices.

The Crane Wife is a tragic story: Supernatural or not, it is about two people with different worldviews and values who cannot find a middle ground and overcome their difficulties, even though they love each other.

Hagoromo

Hagoromo is one of those folk stories which have been turned into a play—the traditional Japanese dance-drama. Although the stories the play is based on were first recorded around the 8th century, the earliest known performance of the play dates to the 16th century (Tyler, 2004).

Hagoromo uses a motif of a swan maiden, slightly similar to that of a crane wife. It's a story about a tennin—a celestial female spirit—who left her feather cloak on a shore. It was later found by a fisherman who refused to give it back to the shapeshifting swan if she didn't perform a special dance for him.

In the play, the swan maiden's dance is the most important part of the whole performance. According to the story, it was a beautiful thing to behold, and it represented the phases of the moon; at the end of it, the maiden disappeared into mist.

There isn't much more to the story; it's more of a scene than a plot, showing a mortal's encounter with the otherworldly and the miraculous.

Hanasaka Jiisan

Hanasaka Jiisan is another one of those stories about a single miracle. It, unsurprisingly, tells the tale of an old childless couple to whom something extraordinary happened.

The couple didn't have children, but they had a dog whom they loved dearly. One day, the dog dug in their garden and found a bag full of gold coins. When the news about this spread, a neighbor came to the couple, saying that it must be proof of the dog having the ability to find hidden treasure. He begged the couple to lend him the animal for only one day, so it could sniff around and dig in his own garden. Reluctantly, the couple agreed.

But when the dog went on the reconnaissance round, it only found some old bones. Enraged, the neighbor kicked the poor animal so hard that he killed it. But he wasn't going to tell the truth to the couple. Instead, he claimed that the dog had just dropped dead; it must have been sick.

The couple wept profusely for their friend and companion, and buried it in their garden, in the exact spot where it had found the gold. That night, the dog's master had a dream: The dog came to him alive and spoke, saying that he should chop down the fig tree growing in his garden and make a mortar out of it.

The man awoke and related his dream to his wife. They decided to do what the dog asked of them. They chopped down the tree, made a mortar, and then tried to grind rice in it; but the moment they did, the rice turned into gold.

Yet again, their neighbor learned of this and demanded to borrow the mortar. But when he put his rice inside, it turned into rotting berries. Again, furious, the man threw the mortar to the ground and then burned it for good measure.

But then, the dog's master had another dream. The dog told him to sprinkle its ashes on the cherry trees in his garden. When he did so, the next day, the cherries blossomed instantly, even though it wasn't their time of the year.

As it happened, a local daimyō was passing by the house. When he saw the beautiful cherry blossoms in the garden, he marveled and gave the old couple lavish gifts for such a beautiful display.

Yet again, the neighbor tried to replicate the same deed that the couple had done, but when he tried to sprinkle his cherry trees with the dog's ashes, a wind picked up and blew the ashes straight into the daimyō's face; for that, he was thrown into prison. When he finally got out, he no longer had a house, and the inhabitants, having discovered his past transgressions, threw him out of their village. Thus, justice was served.

Kachi-kachi Yama

Kachi-kachi Yama is another folktale with a tanuki as a main character; but instead of being the usual harmless trickster, he is the villain of the story. The title can be translated as "Fire-Crackle Mountain," since it is the landmark near which the story takes place, and provides an important plot point to the tale.

One day, there was a farmer whose fields were being repeatedly plundered by a tanuki. Having endured months of this, the man finally came to a breaking point and managed to catch the tanuki and tie it to a tree. He wanted to kill it and cook it for dinner.

But later that day, the farmer's wife passed by the tree. The tanuki started crying and screaming, begging the woman to set him free, and in exchange, he would help her make mochi, a rice dish which she was supposed to prepare. The woman agreed to free the tanuki, only for the malicious creature to immediately kill her.

But this wasn't the end of the creature's maliciousness. He shapeshifted into the form of the now-dead farmer's wife, went to the farmer's home, and cooked some soup. But it wasn't just any soup; he used the flesh of the dead woman to make it.

And thus, the tanuki completed his terrible revenge. When the farmer ate the soup, he turned back to his natural form and revealed the full extent of his scheme. Then, he ran away, leaving the man in utter shock, grief, and mortification.

But the story was by no means over. Now, as the news spread of the tanuki's terrible deed, a rabbit, who had been a neighbor and a friend to the farmer and his wife, came over and promised the man that he would avenge his wife's death.

The rabbit was clever: He didn't just plan out the damage he would cause the tanuki; first, he pretended to befriend him. Only when the tanuki trusted him and let him into his confidence, did he start playing cruel tricks on him.

For example, he once sneakily threw a full bee's nest on the tanuki's head. The bees stung him painfully, and when he asked his 'friend' for help, the rabbit rubbed in ointment made of spicy peppers, thus making the wounds even worse.

But then, the rabbit played an especially cruel trick on the tanuki. One day, the tanuki was carrying some sticks for the fireplace in his home. Unbeknownst to him, the rabbit had set fire to the kindling, but the tanuki didn't notice, since it was strapped to his back.

However, after some time of walking, he heard a crackling sound. He asked the rabbit if he could hear it, too. The rabbit feigned innocence, telling the tanuki that they were passing close to Kachi-Kachi Yama, the fire-breathing mountain that made a crackling noise. No wonder the tanuki was hearing it.

When the flames reached the tanuki's fur, it was already too late to put them out. The creature was burned badly—however, he was still alive, and writhing in agony.

Now, the tanuki knew that the rabbit was no real friend. Having licked his wounds, he challenged the rabbit to a contest; the one who lost would also lose his life.

For the challenge, both creatures built boats that would allow them to traverse a lake. The tanuki, even though manipulative and clever, lacked wisdom, and made his boat out of mud, while the cleverer rabbit made his boat out of a tree trunk.

Even so, the competitors were evenly matched in the beginning; but soon, the tanuki's boat started dissolving in the water. The rabbit stopped paddling in his canoe and turned, satisfaction written in his features: He had achieved his revenge. He then proclaimed that the whole point of the rivalry had been to avenge the farmer—and paddled away, leaving the tanuki to sink. The story ends with the rabbit coming to the farmer's house and announcing that he had achieved his goal. The farmer thanked him profusely, and they remained fast friends till the end of his days.

Kasa Jizō

Kasa Jizō is probably the most Buddhist of tales told in this chapter, aimed at teaching its followers the value of kindness. It starts with a well-known premise: A poor old couple who shows generosity to a supernatural being.

The couple lived in the snowy part of the country, and because of their poverty, would often not even be able to afford some basic kindling. As the day of the New Year was approaching, they realized that they couldn't even afford to make the traditional rice meal, mochi.

The old man decided to try everything. He took some homemade bamboo hats, called kasa, and walked down to the nearest village to sell them. But the road to the village was long, and a blizzard was coming. Soon, the man couldn't even move an inch, and he decided to come back home—only, he didn't even know which direction his home was anymore.

So he walked blindly until suddenly, he almost bumped into holy statues. After a moment, he recognized them as the statues of Jizō, the protector of the vulnerable. He took out his bamboo hats and decided to offer them to the Bodhisattva. However, he didn't have enough hats to cover the heads of all statues; so he took out his hand towel and thus protected them from the snow. Then, he continued on his journey. He finally managed to make it back home safe and sound, and his wife understood why he couldn't bring her the New Year's mochi.

The couple went to sleep. But in the middle of the night, they were suddenly awoken by a thumping on the door. When the old man managed to get out of bed and open the door, there was no one outside—but there was a pile of treasures and food laying on the doorstep. There was mochi, but also vegetables and gold coins.

The old man looked into the distance, where the blizzard was still raging. Faintly, he saw the Jizō statues on the horizon, walking away. They had repaid him for his kindness.

Kobutori Jiisan

Kobutori Jiisan is a tale about an unholy miracle, which was first recorded in the 13th century (Hearn, 1918). It tells the story of a man who had a tumor lump on the right side of his face, and how it magically disappeared.

The man with a lump was a woodcutter. One day, he went into the forest to do his day's work but was surprised by a heavy downpour. He hid in a hollowed-out tree, where he was easily overlooked by anyone who was passing by.

And soon, a very peculiar group gathered outside of his hiding spot. It was a gathering of the on. Some of them had only one eye, and some were mouthless. They soon sat down in a circle and, despite the continuing rain, managed to build a magnificent bonfire. Then, they drank sake and made merry, singing and dancing.

There was something alluring in that gathering, and the woodcutter found himself wanting to join, instead of hiding in a dark and wet tree hollow. After a while, he overcame his fear and let his presence be known.

It was a risky venture, but the demons seemed more entertained by his presence than angered by the fact that he oversaw them. He was a curiosity to them, and they beckoned him to sing and dance with them. After the meeting was finished, the oni told the man to come back the next day. The man agreed, but the demons still wanted a guarantee that he would come back.

So they decided to keep one of his possessions as an assurance. The problem was, the man was poor, and had almost nothing on him—so the demons decided to take away his lump. They removed it smoothly and without any pain, and there wasn't even a scar left. The man was overjoyed.

When he came back to his village, the people immediately noticed the lack of his disfigurement. A neighbor, who had a similar problem—only the lump was on the left side of his face—wished to know everything about the woodcutter's adventure. He then managed to persuade him to take his place the next day, so that he might get his own lump removed.

The man agreed, and the neighbor hid in the same tree hollow he had found the previous day. Like the man before him, he let his presence be known when the oni gathered around the bonfire. But unlike his friend, his dancing skills were not the greatest, and the demons were more irritated than entertained. As a punishment, they not only didn't remove the man's lump but 'gifted' him with his friend's lump instead. Now, he had two lumps on both sides of his face.

This story can be read as a cautionary tale against the envy of our neighbors—but also, as a warning against the oni, whose behavior might be volatile and the contact with whom might not end well for mortals.

Shippeitaro

Shippeitaro might be one of the most famous animal characters in Japanese folklore. The fairy tale about this helper dog has many versions; below, I will present the most well-known one.

There was once a brave warrior who went on a quest for adventure. He entered an enchanted forest and, because he couldn't find the way back before dusk, he slept at a magical shrine in the middle of the woods. During the night, he heard many voices outside the shrine: Cats meowing and wailing, chanting some hymn whose words sounded like "do not tell Shippeitaro!"

The next day, the warrior went to the nearby village. He soon learned that the famed Shippeitaro was a dog owned by an overseer of the local prince and that he was a vicious protector against demonic cats who lived in the forest. However, there was one danger that the villagers believed Shippeitaro couldn't protect them against the spirit of the nearby mountain, to whom they had to sacrifice a girl every year. As it happened, the time for another sacrifice had come. The terrified girl asked the warrior for help.

He agreed to aid her, and he decided to use Shippeitaro after all. The girl was supposed to be locked in a cage and put in the temple where the warrior had spent the night, but the warrior knew that Shippeitaro guarded the shrine. So, he borrowed him from the overseer and put him in the cage instead of the girl.

As suspected, the so-called mountain demon took the form of a giant cat. When he arrived at the temple, it was dark; he didn't see who was sitting in the cage. So, he opened it, and immediately, Shippeitaro jumped out, killing the cat. Once this was done, the warrior joined him, and together they rid the forest of all demonic cats. Afterward, Shippeitaro was celebrated in the village as a hero.

Shita-kiri Suzume

Shita-kiri Suzume is a story about friendship, jealousy, and greed. It starts where most Japanese fables do: With an old couple. The old man was a woodcutter who earned his living honestly and never complained about his lot in life. His wife, however, was greedy and of a malicious disposition.

One day, as the man was cutting wood, he noticed an injured sparrow lying on the ground. He took pity on the poor animal and took it home, where he fed it some rice in hopes that it could help the bird to recover.

But when the man's wife saw this, she was angry. The man was wasting precious food on some insignificant creature, she said. They had an argument, but the man didn't stop caring for the bird.

But the next day, the man had to go back to work. He left the bird in his wife's care, but she had no intention of feeding it. Instead, she went out fishing. As she was gone, the bird, who was slowly recovering, hopped around the house and found a sash full of starch, which it ate. When the woman came back home and noticed this, she got so angry that she cut out the bird's tongue and kicked it out of the house.

When the man came back home, his wife told him what happened. Angered and upset, the man went out in search of the bird. He asked some other sparrows for its whereabouts, and they led him to its nest. There, he was greeted with honors as the bird's friend and savior.

At the end of the gathering, the sparrows wanted to send the man home with a gift. They presented him with a small and a large basket and asked him to choose. The man was old and frail, so he chose the smaller gift, as he knew he wouldn't be able to carry the large basket home.

When he came back and opened his gift, he discovered that the basket was full of gold. He told the whole story to his wife, including the part where he chose the smaller gift. Unsurprisingly, the greedy wife was immediately angered by the fact that her husband didn't go for the larger basket, and decided to seek out the sparrows on her own and come back with large treasure.

She found the sparrows; they, despite having been treated poorly by her, gave her the basket anyway. However, there was one catch, she couldn't open it before she got home.

But the woman couldn't contain her curiosity. She decided to only have a sneak peek when on the road— unfortunately, the moment she opened the basket, deadly snakes, insects, and other creatures immediately crawled out of it, scaring her to her death. Thus, the punishment for her greed was served.

Tawara Tōda Monogatari

The last tale in our collection is an epic one. It is a legendary tale of Fujiwara no Hidesato, a noble warrior who lived in the 10th century. Several prose narratives dating from around the 14th century have been preserved about him (Kimbrough & Shirane, 2018). In English, his story was first translated under the title *My Lord Bag of Rice* (Kimbrough & Shirane, 2018).

The tale goes as follows: In the Ōmi Province in central Japan, a giant snake was attacking travelers. Fujiwara no Hidesato decided to confront it; but as he was crossing near the snake's dwelling, it didn't attack him.

That night, a beautiful woman came to him. She told the warrior that she was the one transforming into a snake; she had been driven out of her home by Lake Biwa (the largest lake in Japan), where a giant centipede was devouring her kin. Fujiwara agreed to go there and get rid of the monster.

The centipede was truly enormous, and its legs were blazing with fire so that when it descended from the mountains, it looked as if an army carrying a thousand torches was marching down. Fujiwara, not deterred, shot two arrows at the centipede but missed. He then prayed to Hachiman, the god of war, to help him kill the creature. This time, the arrow stuck to its body and killed it.

Fujiwara was rewarded profusely for his deed. The serpent woman gave him, among other gifts, a bag of rice that never ran empty. It was on account of this gift that he got his nickname: Tawara Tōda, meaning "The Bag of Rice."

The story of the brave hero closes our journey of Japanese folklore.

Conclusion

You have now reached the end of the book; I hope this was an entertaining and illuminating journey. As you probably already realized, this overview of figures and stories from Japanese myth and folklore was by no means an exhaustive one—after all, we are speaking of a culture that believes in thousands of gods and creatures. There is always more to discover, and I hope that this book will prove an inciting incident for your own fascinating journey through the Land of the Rising Sun.

From the creator gods in ancient chronicles to monsters from modern urban myths, the Japanese tradition is full of love, betrayal, fear, strange creatures, and extraordinary endings—just at the tip of your finger. I hope that this book will serve you as a guide on your way to discovering even more wonders.

References

Adams, R. J., & Seki, K. (1976). *Folktales of Japan*. University Of Chicago Press.

Addiss, S., Yamamoto, A. Y., Jordan, B. G., Secor, J. L., Welch, M., Wolfgram, J., Fister, P., Lillywhite, J., Yamamoto, F. Y., Foresman, H., Deguchi, M., & Carpenter, J. L. (2005). *Japanese ghosts and demons: Art of the supernatural*. G. Braziller In Association With The Spencer Museum Of Art, University Of Kansas.

Agrawala, P. K. (1978). On a four-legged icon of Ganapati from Ghosai. *Artibus Asiae*, *40*(4), 307–310. https://doi.org/10.2307/3249822

Alt, M., Yoda, H., & Komatsu, K. (2018). *An introduction to yōkai culture: Monsters, ghosts, and outsiders in Japanese history*. Japan Publishing Industry Foundation For Culture.

Alt, M. (2020). *From Japan, a mascot for the pandemic*. The New Yorker. https://www.newyorker.com/culture/cultural-comment/from-japan-a-mascot-for-the-pandemic

Ancient tales and folklore of Japan: XXXI. Yosoji's camellia tree. (n.d.). Www.sacred-Texts.com. https://www.sacred-texts.com/shi/atfj/atfj33.htm

Antoni, K. (1991). Momotaro and the spirit of Japan. *Asian Folklore Studies, 50.*

Antoni, K. (2015). On the religious meaning of a Japanese myth: The white hare of Inaba. *Comparative Mythology, 1*(1), 61–72.

Ashkenazi, M. (2008). *Handbook of Japanese mythology.* Oxford University Press.

Aston, W. G. (2013). *The Nihongi: Chronicles of Japan from the earliest times to A.D. 697.* The Japan Society of the UK.

Beauchamp, F. (2010). Asian origins of Cinderella: The Zhuang storyteller of Guangxi. *Oral Tradition, 25*(2), 447–496. https://doi.org/10.1353/ort.2010.0023

Bocking, B. (2016). *Popular dictionary of Shinto.* Curzon.

Cali, J., Dougill, J., & Ciotti, G. (2013). *Shinto shrines: A guide to the sacred sites of Japan's ancient religion.* University Of Hawai'i Press.

Casal, U. A. (1959). The goblin fox and badger and other witch animals of Japan. *Folklore Studies, 18*, 49–58. https://doi.org/10.2307/1177429

Chamberlain, B. H. (2008). *A translation of the "Ko-ji-ki" or records of ancient matters.* Forgotten Books.

Davisson, Z. (2018). *Yūrei: The Japanese ghost.* Chin Music Press.

Deal, W. E., & Ruppert, B. D. (2015). *A cultural history of Japanese Buddhism.* Wiley, Blackwell.

Dejima Nagasaki: Japan experience. (2013). Www.japan-Experience.com. https://www.japan-experience.com/all-about-japan/nagasaki/attractions-excursions/dejima-nagasaki

Encyclopedia of Shinto. (n.d.). 國學院大學デジタルミュージアム. https://d-museum.kokugakuin.ac.jp/eos/

Ernst, D. (2019, September 26). *Essential guide to Japanese monsters.* Bokksu. https://www.bokksu.com/blogs/news/essential-guide-to-japanese-monsters

Farris, W. W. (2009). *Japan to 1600.* University of Hawaii Press.

Faure, B. (2015). *Protectors and predators: Gods of medieval Japan.* University of Hawaii Press.

Gadaleva, E. (2000). Susanoo: One of the central gods in Japanese mythology. *Nichibunken Japan Review:*

Bulletin of the International Research Center for Japanese Studies, *12*(12), 168.

Goepper, R. (1993). Aizen-Myoo: The esoteric king of lust: An iconological study. *Artibus Asiae. Supplementum*, *39*, 3-172. https://doi.org/10.2307/1522701

Tyler, R. (2004). *Japanese nō dramas*. Penguin Books.

Harada, V. H. (1976). The badger in Japanese folklore. *Asian Folklore Studies*, *35*(1), 1–6. https://doi.org/10.2307/1177646

Haviland, W. A. (1999). *Cultural anthropology*. Harcourt Brace College Publishers.

Hearn, L. (1988). *Glimpses of unfamiliar Japan: In two volumes*. Rinsen Book.

Hearn, L. (1918). *Japanese fairy tales*. Boni and Liveright.

Hearn, L. (2020). *The romance of the Milky Way*. BoD – Books on Demand.

Henshall, K. G. (2012). *A history of Japan: From Stone Age to superpower*. Palgrave Macmillan.

Henshall, K. G. (2014). *Historical dictionary of Japan to 1945*. The Scarecrow Press.

Holland, O., & Kobayashi, C. (n.d.). *Japan's ancient and mysterious royal regalia*. CNN.

https://www.cnn.com/style/article/japan-enthronement-royal-regalia/index.html

Holmes, Y. (2014). *Chronological evolution of the Urashima Tarō story and its interpretation.*

Immoos, T., & Ikeda, H. (1973). A type and motif index of Japanese folk-literature. *Monumenta Nipponica, 28*(2), 255. https://doi.org/10.2307/2383873

Jun'ichi, I., & Thal, S. E. (2000). Reappropriating the Japanese myths: Motoori Norinaga and the creation myths of the Kojiki and Nihon Shoki. *Japanese Journal of Religious Studies, 27*(1/2).

Kahara, N. (2004). From folktale hero to local symbol: The transformation of Momotaro (the Peach Boy) in the creation of a local culture. *Waseda Journal of Asian Studies, 25,* 35–61.

Keene, D. (1993). *Seeds in the heart: Japanese literature from earliest times to the late sixteenth century.* Henry Holt & Co.

Kimbrough, R. K. (2006). Translation: The tale of the Fuji Cave. *Japanese Journal of Religious Studies, 33*(2), 337–377. https://doi.org/10.18874/jjrs.33.2.2006.1-22

Kimbrough, K., & Shirane, H. (2018). *Monsters, animals, and other worlds: A collection of short medieval Japanese tales.* Columbia University Press.

von Krenner, W. G. (2013). *Aikido ground fighting: Grappling and submission techniques*. Blue Snake Books.

Littleton, C. S. (2002). *Shinto: Origins, rituals, festivals, spirits, sacred places*. Oxford University Press.

Lovelace, A. (2008). Ghostly and monstrous manifestations of women: Edo to contemporary. *The Irish Journal of Gothic and Horror Studies*, 5.

Meyer, M. (2016). *Aka manto*. Yokai.com. https://yokai.com/akamanto/

Mitford, J. (1871). *Tales of old Japan*. Macmillan And Co.

Monnet, L. (1993). Connaissance délicieuse or the science of jealousy: Tsushima Yūko's story "Kikumushi" (The Chrysanthemum Beetle). *Japan Review*, 4, 199–239.

Nelson, J. K. (2006). *A year in the life of a Shinto shrine*. Seattle Univ. Of Washington Press.

Nukariya, K. (2016). *The religion of the samurai*. Routledge.

Oiwa. (n.d.). Yokai.com. https://yokai.com/oiwa/

Ozaki, Y. T. (n.d.). *The quarrel of the monkey and the crab*. Etc.usf.edu. https://etc.usf.edu/lit2go/72/japanese-fairy-tales/4848/the-quarrel-of-the-monkey-and-the-crab/

Palmer, E. (2016). *Harima Fudoki : A record of ancient Japan reinterpreted.* Brill.

Pawasarat, C. (2020). *The Gion festival.* Catherine Pawasarat.

Perez, L. G. (1998). *The history of Japan.* Greenwood Press.

Philippi, D. L. (1968). *Kojiki.* University Of Tokyo Press.

Picken, S. D. B. (1994). *Essentials of Shinto: An analytical guide to principal teachings.* Greenwood Press.

Picken, S. D. B. (2011). *Historical dictionary of Shinto.* Scarecrow Press.

Punsmann, H. (1962). Daruma, a symbol of luck. *Folklore Studies, 21,* 241–244. https://doi.org/10.2307/1177354

Reider, N. T. (2010). Shuten Dōji (Drunken Demon): A medieval story of the carnivalesque and the rise of warriors and fall of oni. In *Japanese Demon Lore: Oni from Ancient Times to the Present* (pp. 30–52). University Press of Colorado.

Roberts, J. (2010). *Japanese mythology A to Z.* Chelsea House Publishers.

Sansom, G. B. (1982). *A history of Japan.* Stanford U.P.

Sato, H. (2012). *Legends of the samurai.* Duckworth.

Satō, M. (2017). Transforming an ancient myth into a popular medieval tale. In *Japan on the Silk Road* (pp. 339–363). Brill.

Seki, K. (1966). Types of Japanese folktales. *Asian Folklore Studies*, *25*(1), 1–220. https://doi.org/10.2307/1177478

Selinger, V. R. (2013). *Authorizing the shogunate: Ritual and material symbolism in the literary construction of warrior order*. Brill.

Sensitivity of fish to earthquakes. (1933). Nature, 132(3343), 817–817. https://doi.org/10.1038/132817b0

Smyers, K. A. (1996). "My own Inari": Personalization of the deity in Inari worship. *Japanese Journal of Religious Studies*, *23*(1-2), 427–452. https://doi.org/10.18874/jjrs.23.1-2.1996.85-116

Szostak, J. D. (2013). *Painting circles: Tsuchida Bakusen and Nihonga collectives in early twentieth century Japan*. Brill.

Theodore, W., Gluck, C., Tiedemann, A. E., & Dykstra, Y. K. (2001). *Sources of Japanese tradition*. Columbia University Press.

Totman, C. D. (2014). *A history of Japan*. John Wiley & Sons.

Totman, C. D. (2008). *Japan before Perry: A short history.* University Of California Press.

Turnbull, S. R. (2006). *Samurai: The world of the warrior.* Osprey.

Turner, P., & Coulter, C. R. (2001). *Encyclopedia of ancient deities.* Oxford University Press.

Wheeler, P. (2013). *The sacred scriptures of the Japanese.* Henry Schuman.

Varley, H. P. (1977). *Japanese culture: A short history.* Holt, Rinehart And Winston.

de Visser, M. W. (1908). The Tengu. *Transactions of the Asiatic Society of Japan., 36*(3), 107–116.

Yotsuya Kaidan. (n.d.). Www.kabuki21.com. http://www.kabuki21.com/yotsuya_kaidan.php

Made in United States
Troutdale, OR
12/20/2023

16183951R00127